GH STRETTON ROBYN HOLMES ROLF de HEER JUDITH BRETT PETER SPEARRITT MARTIN FLANAGAN STEPHEN N
OWSE VERONICA BRADY SARAH MACDONALD RACHAEL TREASURE GEOFFREY ROBERTSON

ANGELA GOODE ELIZABETH FARRELLY MIRIAM ESTENSEN PETER STANLEY

ROSS McMULLIN TIM MURRAY JULIE RIGG LINCOLN HALL MARGOT RILEY

RTIN ANN CURTHOYS HAZEL ROWLEY KATHY LETTE MOHAMED KHADRA

TTA BARRY JONES DAVID SALTER AKIRA ISOGAWA ROY MASTERS **CHESTE**

LANGTON **TONY DAVIS** ASHLEY HAY TOM KENEALLY PETER KIRKPATRICK

WARDS HUGH STRETTON ROBYN HOLMES ROLF de HEER JUDITH BRETT MARTIN FLANAGAN

EN TIM ROWSE VERONICA BRADY **SARAH MACDONALD** RACHAEL TREASURE **GEOFFREY ROBERTSON** MAGGIE B

I **PERKINS** ANGELA GOODE ELIZABETH FARRELLY MIRIAM ESTENSEN PETER STANLEY SYLVIA LAWSON RUTH W

HRANE ROSS McMULLIN TIM MURRAY JULIE RIGG LINCOLN HALL MARGOT RILEY ELIZABETH WEBBY JOHN HIF

RTIN ANN CURTHOYS HAZEL ROWLEY KATHY LETTE MOHAMED KHADRA DAVID STRATTON HUMPHREY McQUEE

TTA BARRY JONES DAVID SALTER AKIRA ISOGAWA ROY MASTERS CHESTER PORTER JIM DAVIDSON RICHARD W

LANGTON TONY DAVIS ASHLEY HAY TOM KENEALLY PETER KIRKPATRICK MATTHEW EVANS ROBYN ARCHER PET

WARDS HUGH STRETTON ROBYN HOLMES ROLF de HEER JUDITH BRETT PETER SPEARRITT MARTIN FLANAGAN

EN TIM ROWSE VERONICA BRADY SARAH MACDONALD RACHAEL TREASURE GEOFFREY ROBERTSON MAGGIE BE

I PERKINS ANGELA GOODE ELIZABETH FARRELLY **MIRIAM ESTENSEN** PETER STANLEY SYLVIA LAWSON RUTH W

HRANE ROSS McMULLIN TIM MURRAY JULIE RIGG LINCOLN HALL MARGOT RILEY ELIZABETH WEBBY JOHN HIR

RTIN ANN CURTHOYS HAZEL ROWLEY KATHY LETTE MOHAMED KHADRA DAVID STRATTON HUMPHREY McQUEE

TTA BARRY JONES DAVID SALTER AKIRA ISOGAWA **ROY MASTERS** CHESTER PORTER JIM DAVIDSON RICHARD W

LANGTON TONY DAVIS ASHLEY HAY TOM KENEALLY PETER KIRKPATRICK MATTHEW EVANS ROBYN ARCHER PET

WARDS HUGH STRETTON ROBYN HOLMES ROLF de HEER JUDITH BRETT **PETER SPEARRITT** MARTIN FLANAGAN

N TIM ROWSE VERONICA BRADY SARAH MACDONALD RACHAEL TREASURE GEOFFREY ROBERTSON MAGGIE BEE

I PERKINS ANGELA GOODE ELIZABETH FARRELLY MIRIAM ESTENSEN **PETER STANLEY** SYLVIA LAWSON RUTH W

HRANE ROSS McMULLIN TIM MURRAY JULIE RIGG LINCOLN HALL MARGOT RILEY ELIZABETH WEBBY JOHN HIF

RTIN ANN CURTHOYS HAZEL ROWLEY KATHY LETTE MOHAMED KHADRA DAVID STRATTON HUMPHREY McQUEE

TTA BARRY JONES DAVID SALTER AKIRA ISOGAWA ROY MASTERS CHESTER PORTER JIM DAVIDSON RICHARD W

RCIA LANGTON TONY DAVIS ASHLEY HAY TOM KENEALLY PETER KIRKPATRICK MATTHEW EVANS ROBYN ARCHE

WARDS HUGH STRETTON ROBYN HOLMES ROLF de HEER JUDITH BRETT PETER SPEARRITT MARTIN FLANAGAN

EN TIM ROWSE VERONICA BRADY SARAH MACDONALD RACHAEL TREASURE GEOFFREY ROBERTSON MAGGIE BE

PERKINS ANGELA GOODE ELIZABETH FARRELLY MIRIAM ESTENSEN PETER STANLEY SYLVIA LAWSON RUTH WA

RANE ROSS McMULLIN TIM MURRAY JULIE RIGG LINCOLN HALL MARGOT RILEY ELIZABETH WEBBY JOHN HIRS

RTIN ANN CURTHOYS HAZEL ROWLEY **KATHY LETTE** MOHAMED KHADRA DAVID STRATTON HUMPHREY McQUEE

TTA **BARRY JONES** DAVID SALTER AKIRA ISOGAWA ROY MASTERS CHESTER PORTER **JIM DAVIDSON** RICHARD W

RCIA LANGTON TONY DAVIS ASHLEY HAY TOM KENEALLY PETER KIRKPATRICK MATTHEW EVANS ROBYN ARCHE

WARDS HUGH STRETTON ROBYN HOLMES ROLF de HEER JUDITH BRETT PETER SPEARRITT MARTIN FLANAGAN

N TIM ROWSE **VERONICA BRADY** SARAH MACDONALD RACHAEL TREASURE GEOFFREY ROBERTSON MAGGIE BE

I PERKINS ANGELA GOODE ELIZABETH FARRELLY MIRIAM ESTENSEN PETER STANLEY SYLVIA LAWSON RUTH WA

RANE ROSS McMULLIN **TIM MURRAY** JULIE RIGG LINCOLN HALL MARGOT RILEY ELIZABETH WEBBY JOHN HIR

RTIN **ANN CURTHOYS** HAZEL ROWLEY KATHY LETTE MOHAMED KHADRA DAVID STRATTON HUMPHREY McQUEE

TTA BARRY JONES DAVID SALTER AKIRA ISOGAWA ROY MASTERS CHESTER PORTER JIM DAVIDSON RICHARD W

ANGTON TONY DAVIS ASHLEY HAY TOM KENEALLY PETER KIRKPATRICK **MATTHEW EVANS** ROBYN ARCHER PET

WARDS HUGH STRETTON ROBYN HOLMES ROLF de HEER JUDITH BRETT PETER SPEARRITT MARTIN FLANAGAN

N TIM ROWSE VERONICA BRADY SARAH MACDONALD **RACHAEL TREASURE** GEOFFREY ROBERTSON MAGGIE BE

PERKINS ANGELA GOODE ELIZABETH FARRELLY MIRIAM ESTENSEN PETER STANLEY SYLVIA LAWSON RUTH WA

HRANE ROSS McMULLIN TIM MURRAY **JULIE RIGG** LINCOLN HALL MARGOT RILEY ELIZABETH WEBBY JOHN HIR

RTIN ANN CURTHOYS HAZEL ROWLEY KATHY LETTE MOHAMED KHADRA DAVID STRATTON HUMPHREY McQUEE

TA BARRY JONES DAVID SALTER AKIRA ISOGAWA ROY MASTERS CHESTER PORTER JIM DAVIDSON RICHARD W

greats

AUSTRALIAN

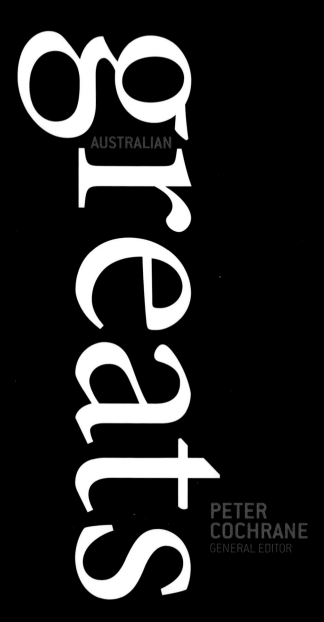

AUSTRALIAN

greats

PETER
COCHRANE
GENERAL EDITOR

WILLIAM HEINEMANN: AUSTRALIA

contents

introduction

PETER COCHRANE

There was a time, not so long ago, when talented Australians departed these shores in droves, certain that everything here was sub par. Greatness, whatever its mysterious content, was somewhere else. We lived with the haunting suspicion that life on this vast continent of ours was rather thin and superficial. So much has changed since then. The way we see the world and the way the world sees us. Clive James expressed this shift in his inimitable way: 'Once the British were astonished when Jack Brabham conquered them in a car he designed himself. Now, when Elle Macpherson conquers them in a bra she designed herself they regard it as perfectly normal.'

Somewhere in between these triumphs, Clive conquered England too.

It is hard to pinpoint the turnaround because it was not simply a moment in time but a process over time. In this collection, John Hirst's essay on Australian nationhood amends our history by telling us that national sentiment, or at least the desire to be something more than *colonial*, was inspired and strong, long before Federation in 1901. And Jim Davidson reminds us how the theatrical whirl in Europe at that time was utterly wowed by our very own Dame Nellie Melba, who operated somewhat like a colonising power in her own right. Yet, as Peter Stanley writes, it was the heroism and sense of imminent threat of Kokoda in 1942 that focused and fired our attachment to this place like nothing before, giving us new understanding of dispossession – of what we might lose and what

Aboriginal people had already lost. The greatness of Judith Wright's life comes in part from this wartime experience – from her love of the land and the sorrows of human atrocity, as Veronica Brady explains.

But we mustn't overstate the link between Australian achievement and merely being here. After all, Sidney Nolan spent most of his creative years abroad; Christina Stead lived not in Australia but in an 'ocean of story', while Patrick White came home from the Middle East and London, but never settled comfortably. And Nick Cave, of course, still comes and goes, with lyrics, scripts and performances that fire up an international audience.

Much of what is great in Australia was inherited from European traditions and practice, mixed into the sunlight of our southern being. This point recurs again and again in the chapters that follow. As Barry Jones explains, our greatest scientist, Macfarlane Burnet, was inspired by Charles Darwin, while Peter Kirkpatrick dubs Henry Lawson 'our first truly modern author', linking him as much with Baudelaire as *The Bulletin* tradition. Yet from this well of inspiration comes a wry humour that could only be Australian. 'Death,' said Lawson, 'is about the only cheerful thing in the bush.'

We are the imagined continent, that unknown southern land, that 'fantasy island' on which sixteenth-century map-makers and navigators imposed their dreams, imagining the land rich with gold, spices and other desirables. Nothing seems further from this pristine fantasy than our foundations as a convict society, and yet there is an extraordinary story here. Convictism is the source of much that is prized in Australia, not least the humour, the larrikinism and the 'fair go' we still value so highly. As one wag put it, 'Australia is marked for glory for its people have been chosen by the finest judges in England.'

Most importantly, convictism was not slavery. Redemption surfaced quickly through opportunity, vision, hard work and ardent ambition. In exile and servitude we find the beginnings, paradoxically, of a British inheritance that bequeathed us Shakespeare's language, the Common Law, the Westminster parliamentary system, sophisticated science, a reliable legal and industrial framework, a cohesive society (by any measure), and a habit of mind that is flexible, adaptive, creative and scornful of authority without substance – traits that came straight out of the Industrial Revolution.

In so many ways we are a conundrum, derivative yet unique. We see this in our institutions; we hear it even in the language we speak – Australian English. As Ruth Wajnryb explains, 'digger' came from the US and 'dinkum' from Britain. Then again, you can take a word like 'mate' and only in Australia will your audience appreciate the multiple meanings it carries, or the 'particular contextual emotion' any one of those meanings might convey, as Tom Keneally explains in his chapter on mateship.

Revolving in the global churn, we have borrowed ideas freely, shaped them to our ends and, in turn, taken new ideas, new stories, new sounds and more to the world. The FX Holden was fashioned after a discarded design for a Chevrolet. Tony Davis breaks this shocking news in his chapter 'Holden Number One'. But the manufacturing made the vehicle ours. When the first FX rolled off the assembly line at Fishermans Bend in Melbourne in 1948, it was a thoroughly Australian product – egalitarian in price, unfussy in accoutrements, and built to withstand our harsh geography.

The 'greats' recorded here fall under a wide range of subject headings – literature, music, science, sport, politics, public service, popular culture, exploration, broadcasting, fashion, cuisine, history, archaeology and language or, to be precise, the Aussie vernacular. Some of the absences are truly shocking – no Phar Lap! – while a number of selections are true blue: Aussie Rules, Nancy Wake, 'Aunty', the BBQ, the humble meat pie. Some remind us that greatness is a complicated condition that can flourish in the midst of ecstatic joy or perpetual grumpiness or utter misery – high achievement often has its price.

There is a contrarian streak here as well. A dog, the kelpie, lovingly portrayed by Angela Goode, leads off. Humphrey McQueen recalls the importance of the 'smoko'. Ann Curthoys' memoir on the Freedom Ride of 1965 tells of courage and commitment to civil rights and the fair go in the face of primitive prejudices in the bush; and Geoffrey Robertson speaks up for Thomas Curnow, the brave schoolteacher who confounded Ned Kelly's plans to wreck a train and kill people. Our best literature points to the tensions that frame us and everything we strive for – between harshness and beauty, meanness and generosity, subservience and larrikinism, indifference and ingenuity.

Reviewing all fifty-three contributions, one is immediately struck by many serendipitous connections. Starting deep in time past, there is a sublime connection, I believe, between the creation myth of Rolf de Heer's chapter and the understandings Tim Murray draws from Lake Mungo. More recently – we're talking some 40,000 years on – the Sydney Opera House and the Harbour Bridge express a people's aspirations across generations; Paul Keating's Redfern speech (1992) joins Robert Menzies' 'Forgotten People' broadcast (1942) as a text that changed the political landscape; Raymond Longford's *The Sentimental Bloke* (1919) and Peter Weir's *Picnic at Hanging Rock* (1975) are linked across generations by exquisite charm and impact way beyond their own time. The Adelaide Festival picks up and extends a love of the arts that is also a legacy of the ABC. The Aussie backyard and the 'barbie' complement one another; so do the chapters on kelpies and wool, on mates and the meat pie, on Chesty Bonds and Speedos, on immunology and peptic ulcers. Finally, Melba and Peter Sculthorpe register as national greats and yet remind us how much this nation has changed – one was an icon of the white Empire while the other is the sound of multicultural Australia.

This book will have served its purpose if it prompts you to make your own list of greats and to ponder the connections between them; to argue about who or what should be on the list and who or what should not, and through that process to penetrate the considerable majesty of Australian achievement. ■

our kelpies

ANGELA GOODE

Our country town has poshed itself up with cafés on the street for a touch of cosmopolitan style. A livestock truck rumbles past and illusions of suave urbanity are rudely shattered by a couple of kelpies, their heads hanging out of dog boxes, hurling abuse along the entire length of the main street. Anyone who might have thought they were sipping in a bit of European sophistication gets a reminder that delusions of grandeur don't mix well with kelpies. These, the greatest of Australia's workers, don't give a hoot about mannered society. Silken paddock skills aside, they pee on the polished boot of pomposity. Canine blue collar workers, they keep their feet on the ground, and those of everyone around them too.

Follow those farm trucks, B-doubles and utes with trailers out to the saleyards and you'll see why working dogs have every right to mouth off. After marking a few tyres while the paperwork is done, they're running across backs, down among legs, emptying pens and knowing their job better than any junior jackeroo. Inept humans daring to interfere will likely earn a look of disdain.

What's so good about working dogs is their wholesome, unquenchable love of work. When the motorbike is kicked to life, they're on the back ready to go. Asked to bring in a mob, they'll speed off casting wide, all lean, silent concentration, sharp eyes anticipating breakaways. In the yards they'll speak up, directing sheep through the drafting race, penning them for shearing or pushing them onto trucks. The best of them almost read your mind. Plenty can muster alone, bringing mobs through paddocks and gateways unassisted, doing the work of two or three humans. From these, the only animals which continue to work large scale in commercial partnership with humans, we learn the joys to be found in hard work. And these workers never hit the grog, rarely go on strike, don't care about holidays, seldom answer back, never ask for a pay rise and scarcely take a sickie.

They're loyal too. Mind you, some dogs struggle to adjust when the boss's single life goes conjugal. They'll get haughty and ignore orders from the interloper, all sullen resentment at being relegated down the pecking order. Then again some blokes say they love the dog more than their wife.

These dogs aren't the pampering type. They might have fancy pedigrees, but they'll bear the scars of fights and toil. City life and daily walks make misfits of them. They're bred tough to take heat, hard ground and big distances. These unfussy workaholics are happy to call a 44-gallon drum home and spend off-work hours digging holes to lie in on hot days. On the back of a ute, they ride like charioteers leaning into corners, eyes blown to slits, pink strap tongues streaming behind.

Kelpies are our own deservedly famous Australian breed, but credit for their genesis belongs to the Scots. Following the Highland Clearances of the 1850s, thousands of immigrant sheep farmers arrived to take up land. These men knew the value of good dogs. Early paintings show they were of no particular breed: black, leggy and lean, or smaller, shaggy and shrewd. Travelling overland with newly bought flocks of sheep, settlers took up land anywhere that reminded them of Scotland. Heat, dust and distance sorted out which dogs had the stamina and strength for droving trips to and from markets – and presumably many failed. In 1869 imported bloodlines from Scotland produced a legendary black dog called Moss for Yarrawonga pastoralist John Rutherford. Further south in the same year, another imported pair owned by George Robertson of Warrock Station, near Casterton, bred a female pup so hotly prized that she was eventually swapped by Ardlethan sheepman Jack Gleeson for his horse. He named her Kelpie after the mythical Scottish creature that would appear in the form of a horse to drowning souls in rivers and fiords. The foundation genes of Gleeson's Kelpie and Moss are found in most good working kelpies.

In 2001 Casterton unveiled a bronze statue to celebrate itself as the birthplace of the kelpie breed and launched an annual Kelpie Festival, held on the Queen's Birthday weekend. With a kelpie street parade, hill climbs, trials and a working dog auction that in 2006 set a world record price of $5,400, Casterton has rather stolen the march on John Rutherford's Yarrawonga and Ardlethan in New South Wales, which also has a sculptural tribute to the kelpie.

While the feats of the champion and legendary dogs are repeated with pride, it's the cold nose of a workmate nudging your arm when things on the farm are at their blackest that often has most meaning. Even if the sheep at times get sent in wrong directions, at least a working dog is unselfish in friendship. ■

sidney nolan

ELIZABETH FARRELLY

For the mid-century generations Sidney Nolan was one of a handful who took
the oxymoron out of 'intelligent Australian'. There were other talents, of course,
other painters; the Boyds and Tuckers and Olsens. But Nolan was different.
Profoundly verbal as well as intensely visual, he joined the demigod gang who
seemed effortlessly to drop smart, funny or entrancingly insightful utterances
into the swirling global conversation with a clear Australian accent. They included
– include – Clive James, Barry Humphreys, Germaine Greer, Robert Hughes and,
more latterly, Peter Carey and Geraldine Brooks. And they are, quite rightly, our
heroes. They use Australia as both base and material but they choose, almost
without exception, to live elsewhere, in what we think of as the world.

It's very Australian, this heroic outsider stance, at once voluntary and
involuntary; something we might even call a national self-image. And it informed
Nolan's choice of subjects, as well as his trajectory. There's Rimbaud, the
iridescently foul-mouthed French catamite. There's the naked and shipwrecked
Mrs Fraser. There's Burke and the decomposing Wills, or is it Wills and the
decomposing Burke? There's self, as in portrait. And there is, of course, Kelly.

So closely identified are Sidney Nolan and Ned Kelly that even the
scholars, many and heavy, sometimes get the names switched, much as a mother
might call Sid Ned, and vice versa. Imagining Kelly, you picture first the black
iron mask from planet Sid, its image burnt into our collective retina with an

intensity usually reserved for film. Only then do you notice the bearded Irish convict glaring out through the slot.

It is this slot that Nolan used to such effect, playing endlessly with both its paintable qualities, as a frame within a frame, and its psychological weight as absent presence. The mask made Nolan famous, and yet it was no more Kelly's mask than his own.

Nolan is revered not just as a painter – though Kenneth Clarke was surely right to recognise his painterly genius and whisk him off to London in the early 1950s – but for *what* he painted: the stories, our stories. And yet he was bored by the bush. Blown away aesthetically by its unutterable beauty, but bored by its reality and even by the characters he so consciously stamped upon it, including Burke and Wills. As he noted in old age, 'I'm masquerading as a narrative painter, on the simple basis that the peasants will understand.'

And they did. Even as the scholars dug away at links to Rimbaud or Spengler or Malevich, the peasants responded viscerally to the stiff dead coppers floating on cerulean skies, the floor tessellated in blood, the burnt orange landscape and the omnipresent soot-black mask, lustrously rendered in Dulux and Ripolin. This populism has at times undermined Nolan's credibility as a fully fledged Modern. Of course, there were the cow carcasses, the deserts. There was death in Nolan. But was he quite uncomfortable enough, wondered the Calvinist critic. Was he adequately pained? Or was he just a tad too pretty, too pictorial, too easily liked?

A more generous or more post-modern view is to see Nolan's populism, be it multivalence or simple marketing strategy, as his Shakespeare aspect: the capacity to spark with equal brilliance on many levels. Key to it, something largely ignored by what curator Barry Pearce calls the 'veritable Everest of opinion' on Nolan, is the eyes.

To enter a major Nolan show is to enter a forest, a universe of eyes. They come in three main styles. There are the leaf-shaped ones, all frontal stare, brilliant white and dead-centre irises, that he slapped onto most portraits and not a few Kellys. There are the round, frog's eggs, as in *First-Class Marksman*, whose glazzies roll towards his prey like yellow jelly-balls along the slot; a slot that is otherwise entirely vacant, washed by the great Spenglerian flux. And there are the small, bruised eyes of the nameless ones, like the grim church-dressed family in *Giggle Palace*, glowering from the Melbourne beach.

And then there are permutations, like the weirdly bespectacled *Young Monkey* that ogles beseechingly from its watery space-womb and the blind, blooded squares-for-eyes of the second Kelly series, where Ned – changed by fire into a Darth Vader Jesus – stares blankly from his charred Laura Ashley Gethsemane.

Is it Christ, then, Nolan's absent presence? Christ, whom Nolan regarded as too literal for art; emblem of love and sacrifice; the ultimate in heroic outsiders. Certainly the suggestions are there, from the cruciform forked animal in *Riverbend*, floating pale and bare among bare, pale trees to the naked Kelly, bareback but still masked, in *River Bank*.

As a child, Nolan intuited this exposed, outsider status, recalling later a sense, in the school parade ground, of 'the atoms, or electrons or something, streaming through me at an enormous rate'. Nolan's subject was neither nature nor narrative, but his own inner landscape, arid, luminous, charred. The mask was his own. Heroic outsider, doomed poet, martyr; it was his mask, and ours. ∎

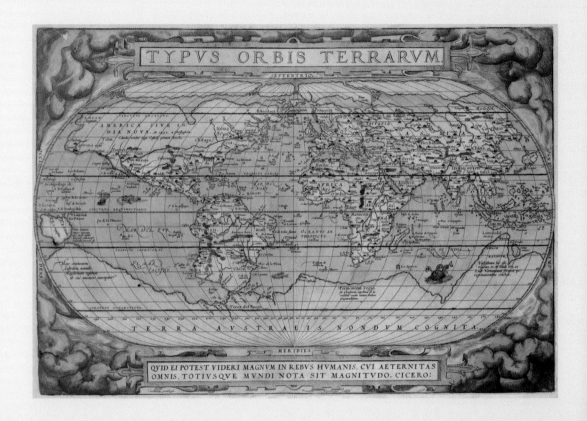

the great southern land

MIRIAM ESTENSEN

In the sixth century BC at the Greek colony of Croton in southern Italy, the philosopher Pythagoras and his followers reached a logical deduction: the earth was a sphere. Logic went further. Because there was a northern landmass of which the Greeks were aware, there had to be a corresponding landmass in the southern hemisphere or an unbalanced earth would have spun off into space. Lost during the long intellectual hiatus of the Middle Ages, the idea was rediscovered during the Renaissance. It was a concept that was to shape the thinking of centuries and lead circuitously to the reality of Australia.

As the intellectual bonds of mediaeval Europe gave way, maritime voyages expanded European geographical knowledge, principally in the latitudes of Europe itself. Below the equator the planet's great oceans remained largely unknown, and here hovered the vision of an unseen continent. Cartographers drew it as enveloping the entire lower reaches of the globe and, reflecting the desires and ideals of the age, labelled it 'gold-producing' and 'overflowing with spices' with an amiable population awaiting conversion to Christianity. Here too was sited Ophir, mysterious source of gold for King Solomon's temple. On maps the gigantic continent was inscribed Terra Australis Incognita, the Unknown Southern Land, or, more confidently, Terra Australis Nodum Cognita, the Southern Land Not Yet Known. Like a lodestone it drew European explorers seeking what did not exist. What did exist, embedded in this immense sweep of imaginary land, was a smaller but very real continent, long isolated by oceans from the rest of the world.

Navigators of the early sixteenth century sailed south but left more questions than answers. The Portuguese Sequeira discovered two islands. Were they Australia's Bathurst or Melville Islands? Mendonça led three ships from Malacca into unknown seas and returned, but no record of the voyage itself survives. On the great curve of southern land, the cartographer Mercator wrote, 'That land lies here is certain, but its size and extent are unknown.'

Spain was in a uniquely advantageous position to seek the South Land. Her American dominions fronted virtually the length of the Pacific Ocean, and tantalising rumours of rich lands to the west circulated at every level from harbourside taverns to the vice-regal court. Thus in the late sixteenth century the Viceroy of Peru dispatched two expeditions into the far Pacific. They found islands – Las Islas de Salomón, Guadalcanal, Santa Cruz and others – but no great continent.

In May 1606 a third expedition reached Vanuatu. Two vessels under Luis Váes de Torres probed the ocean to 21°S. Finding only open sea, they headed north and west through island-studded Torres Strait, the first recorded traverse of the channel between Australia and New Guinea. Did they sight the Australian mainland? We do not know. But Torres had come very close indeed to the reality within the mirage. Unknowingly a little Dutch vessel, the *Duyfken*, had closed that gap, her men landing briefly on Australian beaches. Her captain, however, believed he was on the coast of New Guinea.

Other Dutch ships, travelling north in the Indian Ocean to their trading outposts in today's Indonesia, sighted a long, unknown coastline, which astonished navigators recorded as Terra Australis or New Holland. Two ships under Abel Tasman explored coastal sections of today's Tasmania and New Zealand. Tasmania was clearly not attached to a great southern continent, but New Zealand was probably a promontory of Terra Australis.

For some, the growing reality of Australia was dispelling the mystery of the southern oceans. For others, the vision remained. The French intellectual Charles de Brosses reaffirmed that a vast southern continent was necessary to keep the rotating globe in equilibrium. Alexander Dalrymple, hydrographer for the British Admiralty, published extensive evidence in support of the theory. British ships sailed the Pacific for 'Lands and Islands of great extent', while French expeditions searched the high latitudes of the Atlantic and Indian Oceans. Islands – tropical idylls and cold, barren islets – were the only findings.

The mystery of 2600 years was fading. From 1769 to 1770 James Cook sailed from Tahiti to 40°S and then circumnavigated New Zealand. He found no evidence of the Great Southern Continent. Instead, to a sun-washed land spread across the equator, he gave a known west coast a charted east coast, and initiated a dramatic shift in the concept of a southern continent. Just eighteen years later, exploration began emanating from the continent itself, from a young settlement on that same east coast – brief coastal journeys north and south, Bass Strait and the insularity of Tasmania discovered by Matthew Flinders and George Bass, and tentative land excursions towards the western mountains.

International rivalries between Britain, France and Spain, the personal interest of the influential Sir Joseph Banks and the inspired pursuit of science and reason in the Age of Enlightenment were powerful motivations focusing in a region once part of an imagined world, nurturing in a new society the curiosity and daring that centuries before had carried European exploration into the southern seas. From Sydney's great harbour now emerged the expeditions that finally inscribed the detailed outline of the continent on the maps of the world. From 1801 to 1803 Matthew Flinders circumnavigated the entire landmass and demonstrated on his remarkable charts of 1804 and 1814 that the continent was a single entity, with a geographical unity that made possible the cultural and political unity of a modern nation. Finally, in 1817, the term Terra Australis slipped conclusively into the past as Governor Lachlan Macquarie effectively gave the country a permanent and official name: Australia. ∎

kokoda

PETER STANLEY

In October 1944, two years after the height of the Kokoda fighting, the Australian
writer Dame Mary Gilmore recalled the campaign in her diary. Perhaps she had
been thinking of her young protégé, Andrew White. A promising poet, he had
been killed as a Militia private with the 55/53rd Battalion late in 1942. With
Mary's encouragement, White's verse appeared in a posthumous volume.

Mary reflected on the 'fury that drove our men on . . . driven on by the
fear for the land that was theirs, for their homes and their wives and children,
in case the Japanese reached us'. Their sacrifices, she felt, were 'the measure of
the nearness of our peril', a sense of foreboding that all Australians shared in
1942. Mary Gilmore spoke for Australians in this as in so many things. Many still
believe that Kokoda represented 'the nearness of our peril'.

I had never understood Kokoda. I didn't grasp what happened – that
was confusing enough. I mean I never got what the fuss was about. More
Australians died in Papua than in any other campaign, but surely strategically it
was anticlimactic?

Then one day in 1996 Donald Horne turned up unannounced at the
Australian War Memorial, where I worked at the time. Someone asked me to take
him around. It happened that Horne arrived soon after we had begun thinking
seriously about the re-development of the World War II galleries. We strolled
around the old 'South-West Pacific gallery', me half-apologising for the down-at-

heel display we were about to remove, him chatting genially about his wartime memories. At one point – more-or-less in the middle of the gallery – Horne said, 'Of course, Kokoda's at the centre of it, you know' (or, as they say in army charge sheets, words to that effect). He went on to explain that Kokoda wasn't important because of the strategic significance of the campaign, but because of what it had been like to be there. (He hadn't been in Papua. He'd been a Militia gunner in New South Wales in 1942, later in the Northern Territory.) He talked about Damien Parer, who would become the key to my understanding.

Parer's silent film of the retreat from Isurava to Menari in August and September 1942 shows what it was like to slog up and down those steep ridges in chilly rain, sucking mud and humid heat. He shows us the exhausted, emaciated men, survivors of a jungle battle, the cheerful wounded, the 'biscuit bombers' dropping supplies, the Papuan carriers who made the fight possible by carrying food and ammunition up and wounded soldiers back. However sophisticated our awareness of the power of images to manipulate emotion and understanding, Parer's film seems to show us directly what it was like, and for that he will always have a place in Australian esteem. His genius was to be able to capture a visible truth. Edited by Ken Hall in about a week, Parer's newsreel film *Kokoda Front Line!* opened in Sydney on 22 September 1942, five weeks before Kokoda was retaken. It remains the most eloquent evocation of how terrible Kokoda was for all involved.

Kokoda Front Line! opens with Parer speaking directly to the camera, his face still gaunt from the exertion and privation of the campaign. His words carried all the more poignancy because he was reporting on the feats of Militia men, rank amateurs, the barely trained, 'chocos' or chocolate soldiers as some derisively called them. Parer's shots of these men plodding along slimy tracks and of devoted carriers bearing wounded soldiers on rough stretchers still define the meaning of Kokoda. While he valorised youthful soldiers and loyal carriers, he captured a vision of the truth that informs and deepens our understanding. One scene was staged – the celebrated exploding grass hut – but the entire film exudes sincerity. At the end Parer again stares at the audience, telling them, 'I've seen the war, and I know what your husbands, your sweethearts and brothers are going through.' He ends with the plea, 'If only everybody in Australia could realise that this country is in peril.'

Both Damien Parer and Mary Gilmore were wrong in thinking invasion imminent – hardly anyone at the time understood that the Japanese wanted Papua to protect what they had conquered, and had no plan to keep going. But Donald Horne was right in observing that Kokoda was at the centre of Australia's experience of World War II. Parer's film became the focus of the Kokoda section, in the centre of the new gallery.

That unforgiving terrain and that skilful, tenacious enemy confronted Militia and AIF soldiers with their greatest ordeal of the war, a challenge they met and overcame with skill, courage and an unquenchable humour – as reflected in an exchange between two AIF men:

'Who said those bastards couldn't fight?'

'Who . . . the Japs or the Chocos?'

'Both.'

Damien Parer, Dame Mary Gilmore and Donald Horne responded to the drama, the pity and the pride of Kokoda. They saw why it looms so large in our memory of the War. ∎

Commonly known as the Yellow Book (1962), Joern Utzon submitted
plans detailing the geometrical development and construction of
the minor and major halls and their precast shell lids.

sydney opera house

SYLVIA LAWSON

For almost half a century, the Sydney Opera House has been a focal symbol
of its city and its country. With its external splendours, with all it evokes of a
people's aspirations, with the fraught and contested history of its construction,
the building has attracted writers, artists, architectural scholars and historians
for more than forty years. Long before it was opened with éclat by the Queen in
October 1973, the first argumentative books had been published, the first theses
were being researched.

On 3 March 1966, 1000 architects, students and friends had rallied on
the building site, then marched up Macquarie Street to the state parliament,
protesting publicly that the building's principal architect, Joern Utzon, should
be kept on the job from which he was being forced out. That was the first major
street demonstration of the latter 1960s in the city, predating by several months
the rallies against the Vietnam War, and it was said that the Opera House, as a
cause célèbre, did much to politicise the younger generation.

Utzon and his many supporters lost that battle, bitter cultural war that it
was. The building had been initiated under a Labor government and an idealistic
premier, J. J. Cahill, who lived only long enough to help Utzon lay a foundation
stone. Six years on, with the huge vaults rising into the air and tiling under way,
a conservative Minister for Works, Davis Hughes, put Utzon under impossible
pressure. He made the architect's regular payments conditional on productivity as

he understood it; at the same time he and his department continued to withhold approval for the manufacture of the plywood prototypes that were essential to design and testing in Utzon's system.

That system was always centred on three-dimensional geometry. The work on the building's interiors, like that for the outside, was based on the repetition and mass-production of elements; it can be seen in the segments of the concrete ribs which form the main structure, the chevron-shaped lids which hold the tiles and the tiles themselves. The final roof shapes were derived from a single sphere, with a radius of about seventy-five metres; this enabled great simplicity of both manufacture and construction. Similarly, after much acoustic testing and experiment, the enclosing interiors were to be based on cylindrical geometry. It was always a multicultural story; Utzon's European methods were cooperative, holistic, multi-disciplinary and – in the Australian professional context of the 1960s – unconventional to the point of being offensive.

Thus Utzon got little support from local architects, who understood neither his methods nor the difficulty of the project. He had been briefed to produce a complex in which the major hall would accommodate the differing acoustic requirements of both symphonic music and opera. With the cooperation of specialist acousticians and sound engineers in Europe, he was well on track to solutions for a dual-purpose auditorium. When the government's obstruction brought him to desperation-point, he wrote an ill-considered letter threatening to leave, thus giving Davis Hughes the ammunition he wanted.

The minister took the letter as a resignation, and immediately installed a willing consortium of local architects (Hall, Todd and Littlemore). While Utzon had been accused of extravagance and delays, the new men were allowed all the time and money they wanted to develop new plans for the interiors. They were also permitted to solve the major problem – the dual-purpose hall – by abandoning it. The outcome was the ruptured building as we have it, one in which the inside doesn't understand the outside at all.

The Opera Theatre is cramped and gloomy, the Concert Hall decorated with dated kitsch, and there are constant complaints on the acoustics. The artists who use the auditoria now may not know about the great hall that was planned for both major musical forms, with its stage tower and machinery rising into the high central vault, making full functional sense of that remarkable element. But then and for long afterwards, Utzon was judged lacking in 'practicality'; and so some seven years' extraordinary work and invention, on the far cutting edge of architectural, acoustic and engineering technologies, went to waste.

Now, however, reconciliation is fully in process; there is a renewed recognition that imagination and 'practicality' aren't necessarily opposed. A new conference room is named for Utzon, and a bronze plaque honouring his work stands at the head of the great outside stairway. His architect son, Jan, with Utzon himself, is engaged in work toward a major refurbishment.

So the building changes with time, and with the musical needs of the city. You might be going there for Beethoven or *La Bohème,* for Shakespeare or an Aboriginal dance company. You might use the place (as they did, in March 2003) for an anti-war protest of spectacular resonance. Or you might go there just to meet a friend on the stairway, or to sit around on the seawall in the late afternoon, looking up. ■

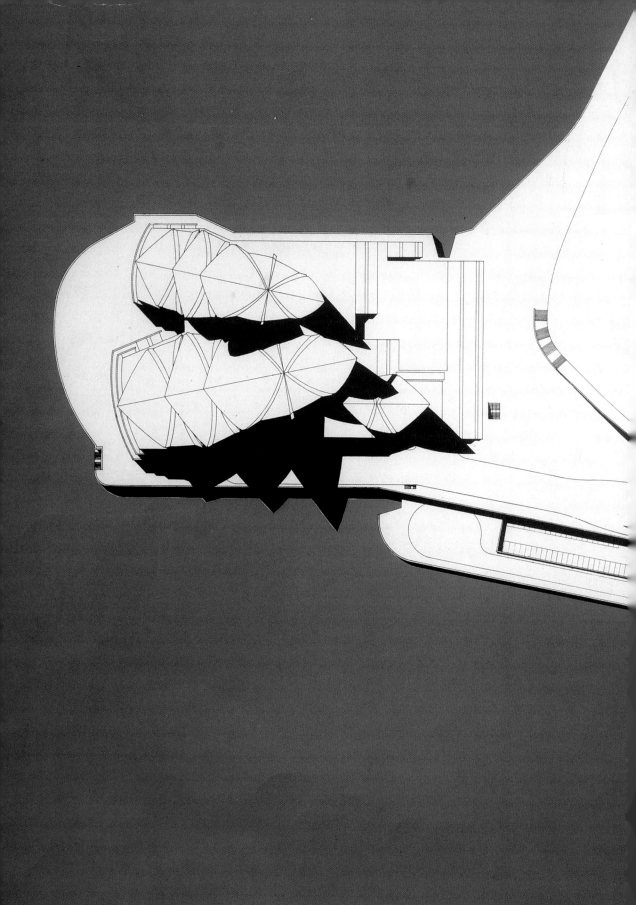

sydney opera house

approaches

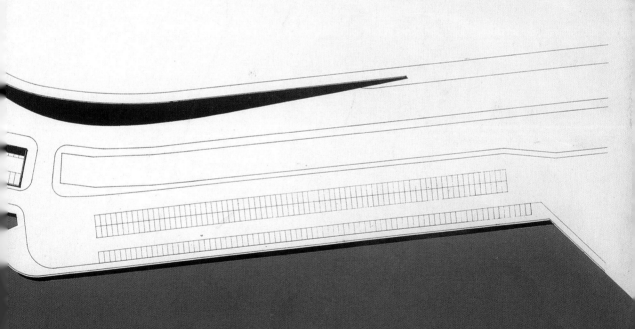

WHEN it comes to slang, the Australians can give us a head start and still win. Their everyday speech is just about the slangiest of all the brands of English.

Both of us, the Australians and the Americans, are young peoples and we like new things—in our speech as well as in anything else. And when someone coins a new phrase, it spreads around in a few days—like "I dood it."

Even more than in ours, colorful, picturesque words and phrases are constantly being added to the Australian speech. Here is a choice selection which may help you to understand what they're talking about:

drogo (a clumsy Australian insect)—rookie
sheila—a babe
cliner—another babe
sninny—a third babe
shivoo—a party
imshi—*amscray*—scram
shikkered—drunk
chivvy—back talk, lip
plonk—cheap wine
smooge—to pitch woo
stonkered—knocked out
boko—nose
shout—to buy drinks for the house

zack—a sixpence
ding dong—swell
yakka—hard work
bonzer—great, super
cobber—pal
wowser—stuffed shirt, sour puss
cow—it stinks
gee-gees—race horses
moke—a plug or nag
brumby—a bronco
billy—tin can for tea
matilda—a tramp's bundle
swaggie—a tramp
drop the bundle—give up
ta—thanks

From the *Pocket Guide to Australia* issued to American servicemen stationed in Australia in World War II by the War and Navy Departments, 1942.

a sandwich short of a picnic

RUTH WAJNRYB

The Israeli novelist, Amos Oz, has commented on ways of knowing other peoples. He says foreign-land travel brings you into contact with 'the palaces and squares, museums and landscapes' of otherness. You come home with postcards, mementoes and memories. But reading a foreign novel 'is a ticket into the most intimate recesses of another . . . people . . . an invitation to visit other people's homes and another country's private quarters'.

It's understandable that the novelist Oz is concerned with the complex web of narrative. After all, the thread from which the cloth of literature is spun is language, doubtless our most precise, authentic, reliable and poignant expression of culture. But it's not only in the literature. It's also in the everyday talk through which we do what we do in the ordinary, and not-so-ordinary, carrying out of our lives. Language is our social broker. It speaks for us, and about us.

Yet the linguistic face of any culture is complex. It's textured and multi-layered, and its richness in most part is a function of tensions and contradictions. Inga Clendinnen has said that in the cultures that humans forge, there's never just the one narrative. There are always multiple strands in the rope and, in a democracy, these get to be spoken and heard. Perhaps the robust, jostling coexistence of multiple narratives is democracy.

Asked about the character of Australian language, we're likely to point to what we think separates us out from other varieties. We chuckle at suggestions our accent's derived from keeping the mouth closed so the flies won't get in – and/or squinting at the sun. We might mention our habit of creating endearing diminutives. *The rellies came over for a barbie and we sat around the pool in our cossies, but the mozzies were bloody atrocious.* It's not always '-ies': McDonald's becomes Maccas; John becomes Johnno; afternoon, arvo. Clearly, we like fiddling with endings. Perhaps, when someone contorts your name into a (usually affectionate) alternative, it's asserting a solidarity, an intimacy. It's congruent with our sense of ourselves as laidback and larrikinish, refusing to take life too seriously.

We're quick to point to our colourful expressions, like 'one sandwich short of a picnic'; or 'a kangaroo loose in the top paddock'; or others in this pattern: 'not playing with a full deck of cards', 'a few beers short of a six-pack', 'a few sangers short of a barbie', 'not the sharpest knife in the drawer'. These feel emblematically Aussie, if only for their topics – beer, barbies, betting, the bush. But we'd be less inclined to believe so were we less monolingual. Germans ask if 'you still have all the cups in the cupboard'; Italians say someone is 'lacking some Fridays'; Poles say someone's 'got a jerky surface under the ceiling'; the Portuguese refer to 'little monkeys in the attic' . . . and that's just a sampling.

There are words we claim are uniquely Australian, ignorant that they've often started life elsewhere. In recent years we have been prolific in sourcing and exploring our 'lexical images'. 'Digger' arrived from the US with the gold rush immigration, some fifty-plus years before it morphed into the archetypal Aussie soldier. 'Dinkum' used to be a British dialect word; even 'kangaroo court' was a borrowing (USA). We bemoan newish Americanisms ('Have a nice day'; 'Enjoy!'), unfazed by those to which we've long acclimatised ('cinch', 'gimmick', 'OK', 'cute'), not realising it's the newness, not the loan, that's the 'problem'. Apart from local developments and Aboriginal loans, and despite much denigration as a 'sub-standard mongrel currency', in the words of Bruce Moore, editor of *The Australian National Dictionary,* Australian English is shared by a world community of English speakers. Its dialectal differences don't interfere with intelligibility.

Still, we have no shortage of expressions that are, well, graphic. Some that leap to mind are 'bangs like a dunny door in a storm' and 'tighter than a fish's arsehole', 'the great Australian salute', and 'as Australian as a meat pie'. We have phrasal verbs that seem to encapsulate large cultural values, like 'dob in' and 'shoot through'; and agent words that say it all: 'dole-bludger', 'bushwacker', 'bower-bird'. Even single words, like 'mate', resonate with multiple meanings, soaking up the particular contextual emotion that enables them to connote anything from affectionate, to cavalier, to derogatory, to belligerent.

But language doesn't stop developing. For a host of reasons, not all of them are the influence of American culture, a lot of these are fading. We have much less need, this century, to be so graphically visual, and certainly less time to squander on what now is considered overly opulent, self-consciously flowery language. The new fashion is minimal and spare: don't waste a word.

Paradoxically, we quickly distance ourselves from the language of the very people, like Paul Hogan and Barry Humphries, whom we've rewarded with iconic status for representing us to the outside world. We recognise their language, of course, but as Hogan's 'prawn (or shrimp) on the barbie' and Humphries' 'possums' fossilise through overuse, they're less and less likely to represent who we think we are.

There's no doubt we revel in our language. As a post-colonial society (albeit, less 'post' than some would wish), it's not surprising we want to distinguish ourselves from the mother tongue, now that we no longer live 'in a world where Empire reign[s]', again in the words of Bruce Moore. But we're in our adolescence: we're being iconoclastic; we're individuating; we're fiercely not-anything else. Language is our identity marker. And like a teenager sporting the latest anything, it's no accident that we sometimes embarrass ourselves.

It's important to remember that though our language habits can be distinctive, the fact that we have them isn't. Like all speech communities, we have particular linguistic ways of doing things. Collectively, it's called Australian English, and it's a dialect in the large, diverse and global family of Englishes. It has more in common than not with the other Englishes, and that's why it's a dialect, not a separate language. But all speech communities make their language do what they want it to do. No doubt the English spoken by the small speech community of Falkland Islanders is also distinctive.

What makes our dialect unique is our attitude to it – our peculiar discomfort with our own attempts to describe our uniqueness. We're a culture chronically and collectively embarrassed about issues of identity; and constitutionally unable to resolve the discomfort. We question, perennially question, what it means to be Australian, a habit of mind that reaches fever pitch at certain, largely predictable times – Australia Day, Anzac Day, political party policy speeches; discussions about the flag, prayers at school, the anthem; Sorry days; citizenship English tests; inserting 'mateship' in the Constitution's preamble; the odd race riot.

Perhaps the day we agree on anthems and flags is the day we cease being as we are, and lose something of what it means, at least currently, to be Australian. ∎

the keating redfern speech

MARCIA LANGTON

At Redfern Park in Sydney on 10 December 1992, one of the most famous speeches in Australian history was delivered by the then Prime Minister, Paul Keating. Keating is credited with bringing the dispossession and marginalisation of Aboriginal people to the forefront of the Australian imagination with the powerful message he delivered at the launch of Australia's celebration of the 1993 United Nations International Year of the World's Indigenous People. He traversed the terrible history of Australia's treatment of Aboriginal people, the need for reconciliation, the Aboriginal deaths in custody, and the very recent High Court 'Mabo' decision recognising Aboriginal native title.

Redfern as the venue was significant because of the high proportion of Aboriginal people in the suburb and their troubled history as Sydney's impoverished and despised minority. Keating asked Australians 'to try to imagine the Aboriginal view'. He said:

> There is one thing today we cannot imagine. We cannot imagine that the descendants of people whose genius and resilience maintained a culture here through 50,000 years or more, through cataclysmic changes

*to the climate and environment, and who then survived two centuries
of dispossession and abuse, will be denied their place in the modern
Australian nation.*

Aboriginal people from around the nation had gathered at Redfern Park that day, and many of its most outspoken leaders were present. There was a mood of hope, tinged with defiance, and the eye-catching flags of the Aboriginal nation flew over their heads – panels of red, black and yellow turning in the breeze. Keating's voice modulated carefully and persistently, but there was a slight catch in his throat as he came to the words that finally caught the attention of the crowd. The buzz of conversation lulled at the end of the first sentence, and all were silent by the third:

*We took the traditional lands and smashed the traditional way of life.
We brought the disasters. The alcohol. We committed the murders.
We took the children from their mothers. We practised discrimination
and exclusion. It was our ignorance and our prejudice. And our failure
to imagine these things being done to us. With some noble exceptions,
we failed to make the most basic human response and enter into their
hearts and minds. We failed to ask – how would I feel if this were
done to me?*

Suddenly, the people responded with outbursts of applause; a few interjected in heated agreement, and a kind of spell – that special magic of great oratory – entranced the crowd. Most Australians recognise those lines from Keating's Redfern speech, because those are the lines that grabbed the nation's attention, just as they grabbed the attention of his audience in Redfern Park. There, all faces were turned toward him:

*If we needed a reminder of this, we received it this year. The Report
of the Royal Commission into Aboriginal Deaths in Custody showed
with devastating clarity that the past lives on in inequality, racism
and injustice in the prejudice and ignorance of non-Aboriginal*

Australians, and in the demoralisation and desperation, the fractured identity, of so many Aborigines and Torres Strait Islanders.

For all this, I do not believe that the Report should fill us with guilt. Down the years, there has been no shortage of guilt, but it has not produced the responses we need. Guilt is not a very constructive emotion.

I think what we need to do is open our hearts a bit. All of us.

There was a collective wriggle of discomfort in the crowd, but the spell of enchantment held. Keating had connected with people who had played the guilt card to wring a bit of compassion from the postcolonial masters, to get funding for medical services, to stop police brutality and deaths in custody, and they knew, just as Keating did, that the strategy was not working. Keating's words were not a rebuke for their efforts, not a criticism of those who had felt guilt and shame as each body was removed from a cell and a small notice in a newspaper published about yet another death in custody. Keating was telling them to do what was necessary, but to do it differently. He appealed to the moral and ethical sense of his nation: perhaps when we recognise what we have in common we will see the things which must be done.

It is an uncomfortable truth for those who felt that the Howard years had undone the good work of Keating's government. It was Keating who urged us to do the practical things, long before Howard commenced his political wedge tactic of turning the nation against 'symbolic reconciliation' to 'practical reconciliation'. The philosophically biting edge of Keating's words lay in this basic proposition: we hold some things in common, whether black or white, advantaged or disadvantaged, and if we recognise our common humanity we will see 'the things which must be done'. He talked about reconciliation, justice and equity, but delivered the rejoinder to these 'meaningless abstractions', used so strategically by people on both sides to evade their responsibilities:

We have to give meaning to 'justice' and 'equity' and . . . we will only give them meaning when we commit ourselves to achieving concrete results.

If we improve the living conditions in one town, they will improve in another. And another. If we raise the standard of health by twenty per cent one year, it will be raised more the next. If we open one door others will follow.

When we see improvement, when we see more dignity, more confidence, more happiness – we will know we are going to win. We need these practical building blocks of change.

This is how he conceived of the link between our higher selves – our ethical selves and our ability to imagine a better future – and our mundane selves, caught in the tragic tide of history. He wanted us to see the Mabo judgment, which brought Australian law into line with modern human rights law, as one of these building blocks.

Keating gave us courage that day. His words were prescient, as some of us continued to mull over the challenge of keeping faith with Koiki Mabo's vision in the face of the vicious backlash – based on fear, hysteria and bald lies – from state governments, farmers and the mining lobby: 'There is nothing to fear or to lose in the recognition of historical truth . . . There is everything to gain.' Each one of us must have felt that he was speaking to us personally, grappling, as we were, with the difficult issues that occupied our minds.

Again, in a deeply touching double manoeuvre, he appealed to us Aboriginal people and to those who had failed to recognise our humanity. With the rank and legitimacy of the highest officer of the Crown, he sought to give us pride in our 50,000-year-long heritage and to snap those who held us in contempt into an understanding of what that meant.

Imagine if ours was the oldest culture in the world and we were told that it was worthless. Imagine if we had resisted this settlement, suffered and died in the defence of our land, and then were told in history books that we had given up without a fight. Imagine if non-Aboriginal Australians had served their country in peace and war and were then ignored in history books. Imagine if our feats on sporting fields had inspired admiration and patriotism and yet did nothing to diminish prejudice. Imagine if our spiritual life was denied and ridiculed.

Imagine if we had suffered the injustice and then were blamed for it. It seems to me that if we can imagine the injustice then we can imagine its opposite. And we can have justice.

With his abiding belief in the goodness of Australians and the strength of our democracy, Keating posed an honourable place for Indigenous Australians in Australian society as inevitable, just, and just plain common sense. He made us believe him, on a sunny day in Redfern on the 10th of December, 1992. ■

This is Holden . . . Australia's own car

It's beautiful, it's modern, it's a car you will be proud to own. And you'll find its practical features more than match its fine appearance. There's performance in the car that will astonish you . . . an acceleration that will challenge anything on the road . . . a sense of security in its handling that makes it a pleasure to drive. Comfort and safety are big features too—due to the Aerobilt single-unit construction of body and chassis. There's ample room for 5 or 6—real room too, with seat width, leg room and head room equal to or better than many bulkier cars. And finally, Holden creates entirely new standards of petrol economy.

holden number one

TONY DAVIS

The tall, rounded body is almost free of bright metal. Inside it's cavernous, Spartan and cold to the touch. A scan of the painted steel dashboard reveals the white bakelite highlights on the handbrake, headlight switch and choke are cracking with age.

But, all-in-all, 'Old Number One' is in remarkable shape.

I turn the flimsy key and push the starter button. The small six-cylinder engine emits a puff of smoke then idles uncertainly. It hasn't been started in a long time and has travelled less than 4000 kilometres in sixty years. And it may never be driven again.

This is the very Holden Prime Minister J.B. Chifley stood beside and 'anointed' before the newsreel cameras on 29 November 1948, the first production example of the modest sedan that changed a nation.

Holden number one was a symbol of hope. It was a pay-off for the pain of war. It was plenty in a time of austerity, proof in-the-metal of how much a young country had learned in six years of hardship.

For generations, Australians have considered themselves Catholic or Protestant, Dragon or Tiger, Cat or Pie – and Holden or Ford. This vehicle stands outside that tribalism. It's the first car wholly manufactured in Australia in profitable numbers. It paved the way for others to be designed, engineered and built in Australia and, at times, exported around the world.

There are myths too, including that Old Number One was the first to roll off the production line. A look at the metal build-plate in the sparsely filled engine bay confirms it: 'Body Number: 6'.

'The story is that it was the best looking body on the line,' says Gordon Adams, a long-time Holden employee who is the car's custodian. 'The panel gaps were best and they liked the colour and they wanted to show it off.'

The second myth is that 'Australia's Own' was designed for local conditions. The Victa lawnmower was based on an overseas design, and the first Holden was a discarded Chevrolet. The Australian engineers were capable enough. They had produced a mock-up of a far more modern car with square headlights. But they were working for a branch office of the world's biggest car company, General Motors, and Detroit had the last say.

Whether through fortune or science, the Americans were probably right. What they considered too small and austere for the US could be adapted for Australian needs and production capabilities and would prove ideal.

Until World War II, General Motors–Holden's had mated imported mechanical components with Australian bodies. During the conflict it built a full-scale foundry and manufactured marine engines, munitions and airframes.

Dozens had previously tried to fully build a car in Australia, many more would yet try. Often these attempts were promising, their products ingenious. But without the sort of plant and equipment that GMH could apply to the task from the end of the war, and without the technical support of a major international producer, it wasn't viable.

The first Holden was codenamed 48-215, popularly known as 'FX', and affectionately called 'the humpy'.

The humpy soubriquet also covers the FJ model of 1953, essentially the same car with a jukebox grille and other minor changes.

In early 2008 – the 60th anniversary year – Old Number One sat in a warehouse at Holden's Fishermans Bend headquarters, the subject of a philosophical argument within Holden. Should it be driven, enjoyed, made to do what it was made to do? Or wrapped in cotton wool and preserved unworn, free from a single stone chip? Those in favour of the latter were winning when Gordon Adams led me to the car, and allowed me to drive a few laps around the plant.

The steering wheel is thin and so large you almost need to stretch out to hold it. The seats are trimmed with a grey material that was believed to be – and may very well be – war-surplus army blankets. The instrumentation consists of a speedo and fuel gauge. To the left is a chrome blank for the optional radio. There was no heater, no turn indicators, just one sun-visor. Armrests were years away.

But engage first gear on the 'three-on-the-tree' gearbox and the reason for the fuss becomes clear. The performance is effortless, and this trait would lead to Australia's enduring love of six-cylinder engines.

The Holden's English competitors mostly had fewer cylinders and smaller, heavier bodies (the Holden had a light and strong 'monocoque' shell). No Austin or Morris could go near to meeting the Holden's boast of 'six seats, 80 miles per hour and 30 miles per gallon'.

The 48-215 is remarkably roomy for its 4.4 metre length. The ride is comfortable and relatively quiet, yet the car was tough too. Owners thumped humpies down unmade roads with remarkably few problems. Taxi drivers loved them.

Adams says the restoration was like an archaeological dig, turning up layers of paint, including blue and green metallics. It's now back to its original Gawler Cream 'Duco', an unremarkable green-tinged ivory that might have been salvaged from the same army store as the seat trim. And the car may soon be stored in a controlled environment, to be wheeled out – not driven – only on major occasions.

Adams calls this car 'the heart and soul of Holden'. His voice literally breaks with emotion when he says it, and he's not the only person who feels so strongly. From it, we gained an iconic brand and, in time, pride in what a new breed of Australian engineers could design, engineer and build from scratch.

More importantly, we gained a car industry, and something to ride on other than the sheep's back. ∎

Plate XXVI

Fitch del et lith.

Vincent Brooks Imp.

Eucalyptus urnigera, H.f.

the mighty eucalypt

ASHLEY HAY

It was one of the most dramatic colonisations of Australia. No one's entirely sure where on the continent it began – this new species had probably popped up in a rainforest somewhere – but it must have looked like a large-scale precursor of Birnam Wood's famous march on Dunsinane. A profusion of foliage spread out into all the nooks and crannies of this place, inching beyond here and there as far north as the land we now call East Timor, Papua New Guinea, to one island in the Philippines. It was 15 million years ago, and the eucalypts were on the move, transforming the landscape with stands of sclerophyllous forest.

Today, if you divided Australia into one-degree sections of latitude and longitude, you'd create 808 squares and find eucalypts in all but 35 of them, their trunks glowing across a brilliant spectrum of colours: orange, rose, silver, yellow, brown, purple, ochre. They may boast bright, showy blossoms, or not; may grow tall and straight and thin, or not; may have rough bark, smooth bark, peeling bark, patterned bark – but they all have a vein that runs around the edge of their leaves, an intramarginal vein. It's one of their distinguishing characteristics.

Now gum trees are so much a part of our definition of who and where we are that we often don't even register them. Perhaps it says something that they'd picked up a European nickname years before they acquired their official botanical epithet, *Eucalyptus*. By the second Australian landfall of Cook's *Endeavour* in 1770, its adventuring naturalist Joseph Banks already found them familiar.

'Most of the trees were gum trees,' he wrote in his journal, and the tag took. It was another eighteen years before a French botanist, Charles-Louis L'Heritier, scooped them into scientific systematics with a proper name and classification – 'eu', from the Greek for 'well', and 'klyptus', for 'covered', referring to the cap on their fruits and buds.

Still, every once in a while, every one of us is pulled up by a eucalypt – whether it's a tree we remember from a backyard, from a painting, from a journey, or a new one that stops us with the shape of its limbs, the thickness of its leaves, the calligraphy on its bark. Once in a while, we still stand and stare at a scribbly bark in case we've hit the one moment when we'll be able to decipher what's written there, to read the story written in its trunk. And once in a while, too, these trees inspire seemingly regular people to grand acts and passions.

There was the Englishman who believed one species of eucalypt would reveal veins of gold; the Algerian resident who believed another could reforest the Sahara; the German botanist who relished another as 'one of the most remarkable and important of all plants in the whole creation!' A young French physician thought they might cure malaria; a gentleman in Bendigo claimed eucalyptus oil had cured his cancer; a group of Italian monks distilled that oil into a strange-tasting liqueur. And Stan Kelly, an engine-driver in rural Victoria, set out to paint the blossoming branch of every eucalypt he could, traversing the country on trains, on buses, on his trusty little scooter, to catch the right tree at the right time, in full flower. By the end of his life, he'd created hundreds of gloriously coloured plates, never quite catching up with botany's ever-expanding list of species.

It's as if there's at least one conversation we each need to have with these trees – no matter all the conversations that have come before. In the late 1950s, the Australian artist Fred Williams came home from the northern hemisphere, announcing his intention to paint the gum tree. You can't, someone remonstrated; 'everyone's done that'.

'Well,' said Williams, 'it's just what I'm going to do.' And it seemed he'd found a way to look through them, paring them back beyond the majestic archetypes and iconographies they'd acquired thanks to artists like Louis Buvelot, Hans Heysen and Albert Namatjira. Of all the eucalypts' incarnations, this one reduced the trees to almost nothing, as if Williams was looking right through the land too, through its light, to reveal these trees as the punctuation among which we live. Look at his paintings – the up-close detail of saplings' trunks, or the open sweep of landscapes around Upwey, along riverbeds, in the country's great warm centre – and you can see the almost human curves of their boughs, hear the wind through those dangling, leathery leaves, smell the distinctive smell of those leaves crushed between your fingers. He caught some identifiable essence from among all their differences, capturing everything about them that's familiar in spare dots and dashes – like 'a Morse Code of tree tops', someone said.

We still use Banks's shorthand for them, our gum trees, and they're a pretty good shorthand for us too, a mongrel mob of various and adaptable Australians, tenacious, and with the poetry of the place inside. As Douglas Stewart said in one of his own poems, 'It's the gum trees' country,' this place. 'They had it before we came, / They'll have it again when we're gone.' ■

Eucalyptus canopy at Mt. Oberon, Wilsons Promontory, Victoria.
Portrait by Christian Fletcher.

mateship

TOM KENEALLY

There is a national assumption that mateship, an intense bond between males, is – in the whole world – most intense in Australia. The word is invoked with such a sense of holiness that it covers our ideas of liberty and fraternity. It was forged in the miseries of convictism, enhanced by the enormous distances and vicissitudes covered and endured by stockmen and shearers in the nineteenth century, institutionalised in the great strike of 1892 and the emergence of unionism, and sanctified in the sacrifices and heroism of wars and their horror camps.

There is no doubt that solidarity and friendship between males is a potentially positive experience – one every male should have if he wants to be well-rounded. Males honour this reality in the way they address each other in Australia. The inclusion of the word 'mate' in a sentence is essential if you wish to avoid the impression that you're being pretentious or hostile. Above all, it's the Australian peace-word between males. Sometimes it works, too, stopping the thrown fist. Mate is also a word for the barbecue, where it can be used three times on its own in a sentence to mean as many things.

'It's a great day, mate!' the host might say.

To which the reply, 'Mate, mate, maaate!' means, 'I greet you in return, I too think the weather's good, and I've had a good week at work, relish the aroma of your snags and exult in the temporary perfection of the cosmos.'

I confess to having used it occasionally myself in all three senses and a few more, though not in the one sentence.

Mateship, when it's Weary Dunlop trying to soothe the nightmares of an Australian prisoner dying of beri-beri on the Burma railway, is a noble thing. Mateship was good even when my old dad was dared by his section of Australian males during World War II to ask King Farouk of Egypt, who was visiting an excavation in the desert, to give them a lift into Cairo so they didn't have to wait for a military truck and all its discomforts. What did they say to my father as they shot along the highway in the king's huge limo? 'You really done it, mate!'

But the assumption is that our mateship is the top variety, that it is superior to the friendships of males elsewhere not only in degree, but in substance. Certainly, as a war-time child, I heard from the mouths of returning diggers that Australian officers in Changi and elsewhere had more concern for their non-commissioned men than British officers did. This was certainly a triumph for mateship based on the idea of equality. Egalitarianism, despite our being globalised and worn down to the homogeneous and pallid virtues of the world at large, is still a principle which we have to make gestures to, and do so unconsciously. British plumbers, when I lived in Britain a while, called householders 'sir'. Australian householders call their plumber 'mate', in the hope of fraternal discounts or better work.

Yet, despite the added quality egalitarianism gives to mateship, there are dangers in considering ourselves especially gifted in it, indeed to have cornered the market in it. It can have a holiness. It can also be a bond of savagery. The convicts and ticket-of-leave men who committed the Myall Creek Massacre in 1837, encouraged by the earlier exploits of their social better, the execrable Major Nunn of the Mounted Police, believed themselves mates. The feral youths trawling the streets for female flesh in the Australian movie *The Boys* considered themselves mates. One of the darkest epitomes of mateship is pack rape. The Cronulla rioters were bound in mateship against those they considered didn't subscribe to that ideal.

For much of Australian history mateship has tended to exclude. Unless an Aborigine was a top stockman or sportsman, they were excluded. And as has been so often scathingly reported, women are excluded. So what does one make of a nationally revered institution which excludes 51 per cent of the citizens of the Commonwealth of Australia? Does it deserve the lustre bestowed on it?

In a lifetime of some length, I have seen mateship painfully and reluctantly expand itself to the post-war refugees, to Asian-Australians, and now to Muslims. The team members of the Sydney Bulldogs Rugby League would not consider their famous Muslim, Ramadan-observing winger, Hazem el Masri, anything but a mate, although it has to be said he had to show his natural nobility and kick goals unerringly to get there.

Even the utterance, 'I've got this gay mate who says . . .' is no longer an impossibility, though generally gay men are still treated with as much undue suspicion at the altar of Australian mateship as they are at the altar of Cardinal George Pell.

So, mateship has been a great Australian democratic virtue, sometimes joyous, sometimes grudging, and a great hysterical Australian vice as well. In so far as it recognises friendship and respect amongst men, I cherish it as much as anyone. Indeed, in a number of social and working situations it has proved an engine of tolerance too. The newcomer of course has to prove himself, but if he picks up on the sometimes unfair signals of the mass, he can find himself addressed as mate and being assured he is not such a bad poor Pommy/Wog/Towel-head bastard. That's the thing. Mateship tends to be a rough implement. Yet it is also true that despite its painful possibilities, it has sometimes worked better than all the invoked fraternity of other nations.

I also weep, however, for the manifold crimes and follies committed in the name of mateship, and for the way women's advice and hope are fobbed off with the cry, 'I've gotta, he's my mate.'

With all these qualifications thrown in, there's no doubting its continuing potency, and the enduring if deluded belief that the bond between male friends on this continent is superior to that enjoyed anywhere else on planet Earth. ∎

henry lawson

PETER KIRKPATRICK

For most of its history Australia has been predominantly a nation of city-dwellers. Yet many Australians believe that, spiritually, they are rural folk whose values of wry humour, mateship and stoic fortitude were forged by the rigours of frontier life.

Through his creation of characters such as Mitchell, the Drover's Wife, Joe Wilson, Steelman and the Bush Undertaker, Henry Lawson was one of the main creators of that belief. For A.G. Stephens, literary editor of *The Bulletin* where his work first appeared, Lawson was 'the voice of the bush', and that's the popular image that has come down of him. His rugged profile once featured on the ten dollar note, superimposed on images of old Gulgong in its 'Roaring Days', as if he'd called the town into being.

But Lawson was a bush boy who mostly hated the bush, and when he wrote from that estrangement he wrote superbly. His literary peers such as 'Banjo' Paterson depicted life up-country, for all its remoteness and hardship, in communal terms. Lawson's best work, on the other hand, explores the lives of isolated individuals who struggle to inhabit, not just a geographical frontier, but often the very edges of reason. It's this that makes him our first truly modern author.

Lawson's restless Norwegian father, Niels Larsen, had been a sailor and goldminer and would vainly continue to seek his fortune after the marriage.

His mother, Louisa née Albury, entertained very different ambitions and would become a pioneering feminist. Henry's childhood steered an unsteady, fretful course between their opposing temperaments. He grew up on a dirt-poor selection at Eurunderee, near Mudgee, where financial woes intensified his parents' marital problems. Niels was frequently absent, working as a bush carpenter, which left Henry – as the oldest child – feeling responsible for his mother and siblings but powerless in the face of their privation. Ever sensitive, he became anxious and introverted. The onset of deafness from the age of nine further sealed him up within himself.

After his parents separated, Henry followed his mother to Sydney. Despite occasional sojourns interstate or overseas, the city would be his home till the end of his days. Here, contact with Louisa's socialist circle radicalised Henry. His first published work was 'A Song of the Republic', where he called upon his fellow Australians to,

> Banish from under your bonny skies Those old-world errors and wrongs and lies Making a hell in a Paradise That belongs to your sons and you.

He depicted the consequence of failing to do so in 'Faces in the Street', in which Sydney becomes just such a hell for its workers:

> In hours before the dawning dims the starlight in the sky The wan and weary faces first begin to trickle by, Increasing as the moments hurry on with morning feet, Till like a pallid river flow the faces in the street – Flowing in, flowing in, To the beat of hurried feet – Ah! I sorrow for the owners of those faces in the street.

It's the personal that's most political in Lawson's poetry, though. 'The Watch on the Kerb' is a plaintive lullaby for a prostitute plying her trade at night, counselling hope in the face of desperation. 'Andy's Gone with Cattle', while it tells of the sadness of parting, also touches on class politics:

Oh, who shall cheek the squatter now When he comes round us snarling? His tongue is growing hotter now Since Andy cross'd the Darling.

In a satiric mode, there's the figure of Middleton's Rouseabout, 'Type of a coming nation', who rises from station dogsbody to station owner, but still 'Hasn't any opinions, Hasn't any "idears"'.

Though his poetry remains popular, Lawson's fiction now attracts greater critical interest. He called his stories 'sketches', as a mark of their journalistic origins. If not a lot seems to happen in some of these laconic tales, they also reveal unique forms of human experience. The Drover's Wife withstands all that the wilderness throws at her – including fire, flood, mad bullocks and dangerous swagmen – and in doing so heroically steps beyond the conventional femininity depicted in her fading copies of the *Young Ladies' Journal*. By killing the snake, which provides the framing narrative, she becomes a redeemed Eve – a new kind of woman behind whom it's not hard to see the resolute figure of Louisa.

In a parody of contemporary anthropology, the Bush Undertaker sets out on Christmas Day to disinter an Aboriginal grave, only later to take great pains in giving the corpse of an old mate, mummified by rum and exposure, a decent burial: 'Hashes ter hashes, dus ter dus, Brummy – an' – an' in hopes of a great an' gerlorious rassaraction!' But the meaning of the words evaporates in the heat. The story concludes:

And the sun sank on the grand Australian bush – the nurse and tutor of eccentric minds, the home of the weird, and of much that is different from things in other lands.

The bush may be what symbolises Australia, but it's also a strange, unsettling place in which Western rituals – and Western forms of knowledge – break down.

Lawson once observed that 'death is about the only cheerful thing in the bush'. This may explain the success of his best-loved story, 'The Loaded Dog', in which an explosive cartridge designed to blow up a waterhole full of fish becomes, in the jaws of a young retriever, 'a big, foolish, four-footed mate', a lethal comic device. As in all good slapstick, the prospect of sudden death underpins the humour but, precisely because Lawson's agent of disorder is a 'mate', nothing bad ultimately happens.

With growing literary fame, Lawson married and tried his luck in London. Both efforts were failures. His attempt at a novel, which became the Joe Wilson stories, only confirmed that he was best in understated, discontinuous forms. As his life began to fall apart through alcohol, mateship became an increasingly strident force in his work, a bulwark against women, the world and his own depression.

Following Federation and then World War I, Australians grew ever more aware that they had entered the modern world, and they became nostalgic for their undomesticated rural past. Lawson's fragmentary, questioning accounts of the colonial frontier were co-opted into a grander story of nationhood: a triumphal tale of pioneers and of progress, unshadowed by doubt about its meaning or dismay at its effects. Consequently, as Lawson's inspiration declined, his celebrity increased – not that that it did him any good. Having been institutionalised so many times in his life, ironically Lawson himself now became an institution. So when he died as he'd begun, dirt-poor, he was promptly given a state funeral.

Lawson bequeathed to Australian fiction a powerful documentary style that many later writers bridled against: what Patrick White famously dismissed as 'the dreary, dun-coloured offspring of journalistic realism'. Yet the settings of Lawson's work are, like White's, as much internal spaces as external ones, expressing the boundaries of European consciousness struggling to come to terms with an uncanny new landscape where the old symbols no longer make sense and must be re-imagined. ■

Anything Vegetarian? by Jeff Carter, 1996. Feeding the masses at a barbecue in Wanaaring, New South Wales.

the barbecue

MATTHEW EVANS

Richard hands the tongs over to the nearest bloke. He's gained a dodgy reputation with the barbecue since that first night when, according to those well-worn excuses, it was dark, raining and his new Beefeater barbie was swung into service. Meat burnt on the outside and raw in the middle. An homage to our fathers' mastery of the art.

The gender rules for this modern barbecue, held in an inner-city suburb, haven't really changed since our parents' time. Richard mans the burners while Liz handles the salads. Men playing with fire, women actually producing the food.

Does today's backyard barbie, that iconic weekend get-together, have the same rules as a free gas barbecue down by the water's edge? Is it okay to make Asian slaw flavoured with kaffir lime and a hint of fish sauce? If you bring organic, hormone-free meat, should you be offended if it's commandeered by the host and cooked with everybody else's?

In the old days barbecue etiquette was simple. Take a salad (potato, green or coleslaw) in consultation with the host. Take all the meat you could eat, plus enough for another two or three souls, and eat that too. And take an esky packed full of ice-cold tubes, along with a stubby holder or three. When you arrived you'd split up along gender lines, boys outside, straight to the hotplate and flames, girls to the kitchen where they'd make mayonnaise from condensed milk, dried mustard powder and vinegar. The boys would inevitably overcook the protein, the lettuce was always iceberg and the kids were given snags, dredged with sugar-laden dead horse, sandwiched in white bread.

Where once the Aussie barbecue, a celebration of smoke and charred chops, tongs and tinnies, was an invitation to bring your own meat, now the line has been blurred. As guests we've brought cool ales, a rosé and Alkoomi's shiraz viognier from Western Australia. No meat.

At least the rules for vegetarians remain unchanged. Bring your own or be prepared to eat the next closest thing to a meatless barbecue: supermarket sausages and salad. For the true omnivore not used to our culture, however, the BYO Aussie barbecue is just plain weird. You wouldn't go to someone's house for dinner and take a roast, says my Belgian-born friend, Anouk – why do you take meat to a barbie?

It seems a peculiarly Australian thing, this BYO attitude. It must stem from the original barbecues, held at riverbanks, the casual free-for-all where six families arrived at slightly different times and everybody would bring their own tucker.

If you ask men my father's age, they'll tell you a barbie was all about the cooking. What kind of timber was used and how much to let it burn down to coals. How much you should char the outside of the meat, regardless of how bloody the insides remained. (And, remarkably, they sometimes did serve meat pink.) How you always used a slosh of beer and a piece of screwed-up newspaper to clean the possum poo off the hotplate, mopping up the residue with onions fried in oil. The cleaning didn't change, even when barbecues converted to gas. Meat cooking, however, is still hotly debated; to prod or not, to turn the steaks more than once, or not. To prick the snags?

Our host, Richard, is relieved to let go of his grip on responsibility when the fish is brought out. It's harder to nail seafood cooking than meat. Two whole snapper are strewn with sliced lemon and wrapped in foil. There's corn, soaked in water to prevent the husks burning, ready to be chargrilled whole. Onions are sliced, roughly, and tossed unceremoniously on the hotplate – though this hotplate looks suspiciously clean.

As the propensity to expect all-comers to bring meat has changed, so has the fodder itself. Today's barbecue may be topped with a banana-leaf-wrapped piece of blue eye or dotted with Vietnamese-style pork balls. The lamb may be marinated in chermoula, sirloin steak dusted with smoked paprika. Chicken has become cheaper but relatively flavourless, so it's sparked up by being marinated in lime and coriander. Eggplant and zucchini are chargrilled, mushrooms too. Whole joints are cooked on covered barbecues, and you can roast a chicken with a tinny of beer up its cloaca, so it steams as it cooks. Juicy inside, crisp outside. Barbie fans are learning to smoke their foods, to brine them so they stay moist, to cook in kettle-style barbecues over red-gum coals.

Today Liz has tossed a peach, prosciutto and bocconcini salad, and dressed chats – baby potatoes – with olive oil and green onion. Richard's meat includes sausages: lamb with rosemary; beef with, well, nobody's quite sure, even after we've eaten it. Not everything has changed. Surprise bags are still a surprise. And, despite strong evidence that we can't be trusted, it seems it's still the men who wield the tongs. ▪

the adelaide festival

ROBYN ARCHER

At an Adelaide Festival in the early 70s, when I was still an entertainer with scant knowledge or experience of art, I felt the 'shock of the new'. I happened upon a naked woman, playing a grand piano on a platform being lowered from a crane against the black night sky over the new Adelaide Festival Centre. A few days later I encountered her naked on North Terrace, playing a cello made of ice, which gradually melted between her legs. I did not know then how to name this woman as an important New York performance artist: all I knew was the thrill of something unexpected , unimagined and genuinely exciting.

In the hands of Anthony Steel, the festival gave Adelaide its first opportunity for such encounters. By then that festival was already ten years old and younger by a year or two than the Perth Festival. Both were created in the wake of the Edinburgh Festival, whose altruistic beginnings as a post-war gesture to peace in Europe had by then faded from public memory. Both were colonial inventions bred from a desire of the good citizens of those far-flung states to have a taste of the culture from which they were mostly cut off. Hence, the Anglo-centric nature of their first programs.

But when the good burghers of my hometown cloned Edinburgh in Adelaide, they did it in the right city. With the advent of Federation Square, Melbourne has with one grand gesture made its arts precinct connected and tangible, yet Adelaide still feels more contained, succinct, 'walkable', and thus the most like Edinburgh of all Australian festival cities. This similarity has prompted Adelaide to follow Edinburgh even more closely: with an enormously expanded Fringe, Womadelaide and the Writers' Festival, we find a conscious replication of Edinburgh's hosting of nine separate festivals at the same time. While a sense of place is central to any festival's unique identity, the fact is that the Edinburgh model works well in Adelaide.

Because the main festival has wisely remained biennial, it can be both anticipated and savoured longer, and this, together with a sense of pilgrimage, has kept it special. This was joyously evident when Peter Brook's *Mahabharata* came to town or, more precisely, to a specially prepared venue to the north-east. Actors and their friends who couldn't afford accommodation took the bus from Sydney, arrived in Adelaide, stayed twelve hours at the show and took the bus back that day. It was an unforgettable night in the suburbs. The epic story of Indian princes and battles, passions and betrayals, had occupied eight hours against the sandy quarry's backdrop: eyes closed now and then, we were borne along in a vivid poetic dream state. As the wars subsided and a sage heralded peace, the first signs of dawn appeared in the eastern sky, and suddenly Indian mythology was gently pierced by a magpie's lush carolling. Brook, and the festival, had got it right.

When I returned twenty-five years later to direct two Adelaide Festivals, that memory gave me the confidence to program Robert LePage's seven-hour epic, *The Seven Streams of the River Ota*. By then it had also long been accepted that Australian work deserved its place next to the international invitations. In 2000 we commissioned twenty-seven new works, which included *The Theft of Sita* (Nigel Jamieson, Paul Grabowsky with Balinese artists) and Yue Ling Jie (Lisa Lim with Elision), both of which subsequently toured the world with splendid success.

These days every Australian state has its own international arts festival and, apart from the newest kids on the block (the Darwin Festival and Ten Days on the Island in Tasmania, both of which have a special sense of place at the core of their programming ethos), they all operate on similar curatorial principles.

They are important institutions in each state's cultural calendar and, funded as such, they have to be fiscally squeaky clean. Therein lies the potential for risk-aversion, which in turn means that the shock of the new is harder to come by. Yet recent studies in neuro-aesthetics suggest that it is precisely by being shaken from the known through an unexpected moment in a work of art that we actually put our brains to best use. All of us, not just art lovers, desperately need what only art can provide. As scientists, architects and economists become the celebrities thousands flock to hear, arts festivals have a huge responsibility to position artists as equally important and their riskiest work as valuable as that of other professions.

At the heart of the audience experience is something much closer to blood and tradition – the sense of excess and over-indulgence which sits at the heart of all festivity. This is why festivals often work better in smaller cities where they can take over, and also why it is so important to do more than just book the sexiest acts on the circuit. The final effect must amount to much more than the mere sum of the parts, and that depends on the creative skills of the artistic director.

In Adelaide the impact is felt in the streets as the festival occupies the city and temporarily changes its character, offering citizens the chance to do the same. A quintessential experience immerses you in the arcane nature of festivals – to go outside of yourself, to indulge excessively and to return to normal life somewhat altered. The ideal post-festival state is one of saturation and exhaustion, having done things that would not have been possible had you not made that pilgrimage from suburb, bush, interstate or overseas. Ensuring that offer extends to a public that may not be able to afford the escalating ticket price to an arts event has placed immense value on those bits of the program which are free to the public: and Adelaide has a ninety-nine per cent guaranteed assurance of warm dry weather at festival time.

Invited to direct the 1998 (twentieth anniversary) and 2000 Adelaide Festivals, I pondered long on how an arts festival could find common ground with everyone – not just arts lovers. What celebration did we all still share in contemporary multicultural Australia at the end of the twentieth century?

Birthdays, weddings and funerals. Would it have been possible to plan *Every Day a Wedding* in any other arts festival? Each dusk in the beautiful old rotunda in Elder Park, next to the mighty Torrens River and a two-minute stroll across the grass to the Festival Centre, we staged a wedding.

Initially imagined as culturally diverse showpieces, more than half became legal ceremonies – a gypsy wedding whose entourage arrived mantilla-clad on horseback, the groom singing flamenco to his bride. A hippie wedding arrived in a purple Kombi van; six gay couples pledged their troth together; and a Scottish wedding bagpiped its way along the banks. Each night hundreds of people came to watch and cry and applaud, and the next day in the paper a critic praised the frocks and the music and the romantic sentiments. On the last night a member of staff married her partner there. Nine months later, to the day, they had their first child. Now that's what I call a festival, and perhaps it will remain true for some time to say 'only in Adelaide'. ■

william charles wentworth

PETER COCHRANE

Some lives are mythic – irresistible stories that once revealed will draw us back, invigorating the past in us, generation upon generation, each round giving up new meaning, confirming a greatness that is undeniable yet, as so often is the case, a greatness that is fragile, suspect, demanding endless reassessment.

William Charles Wentworth (1790–1872) is such a life. He was immensely talented, ferociously driven and grandiose in his ambition for himself, his family and what he called 'my country'. He was among the first Europeans to feel that Australia was his patria, but his vision for this new homeland was oligarchic. After decades of political battle, Wentworth became a red-hot opponent of democracy, his last years lived in bitter exile in London, his country going its own way, lost, he said, to the dirty scramblers and revilers who had snatched power from the deserving men of property and education – men such as himself.

He is remembered as a turncoat, a carouser, a coarse and angry man and a political reactionary. Yet he was so much more. For almost half a century he was central to institutional change and public life in the Australian colonies, most notably in his political base in Sydney. For most of that time he was a scourge to Downing Street.

On all the big issues of political reform – trial by jury, freedom of the press, self-government, constitutionalism and the great question of oligarchy or democracy – he was at the centre of the contest, cursing, cajoling, shaping petitions, drafting law, speechifying, blasting his enemies and vowing revenge. He was a writer, orator and agitator who lived passionately and defiantly through the first fragment of our political history.

Men who are angry, arrogant, visionary and vindictive have been dynamic agents of social and political transformation. Their driven energies have transformed colonies and nations. So it was with Wentworth.

His mother was an emancipated convict woman. His father was an exiled highwayman who made a fortune in the time of Governor Macquarie and bequeathed much of it to his son. In his early thirties William could count himself among the wealthiest of the great landowners of New South Wales. He was with them but not of them. Wealth did not cancel out the taint of convictism, nor did the years soften this great divide. Wentworth was a political leader among men who treated him, socially, as a pariah.

His family, too, were shunned. The insult and derision piled up over decades. Private wounds shaped public destiny. Exclusion became a badge of identity. It defined him, it fuelled his fire. He was a tortured man, hell-bent on having some ultimate triumph over all of his colonial oppressors. His rough-edged, hard-drinking, sharp-tongued persona grew naturally from his early emancipist associations *and* it was a self-styled defiance of his peers. He was the landed gentry's bulldog, and he was the dog that did not come inside.

He had once dreamed he would shape Sydney and the colony of New South Wales as if it were glazing putty in his hands. As years passed and the fight wore on, and as self-government came into view, so close in the early 1850s that he could almost smell it, he began to doubt that he would ever have honour for his family or justice for himself. He felt the future slipping from his grasp. Shifts in the culture, new people, new social patterns, matters of taste and disposition, were subverting his lordly aspirations. He sensed how forces that he despised might prevail – in society, the snobbery and viperishness of 'upper' Sydney; in politics, the rampaging ambitions of the milk-water liberals and those filthy, sock-less democrats.

On 22 May 1856, when the first parliament of New South Wales came together, Wentworth and his wife and their ten children were settled in London. There he shared common grumblings with a circle of wealthy expatriates who decried the evils of the new political system in Sydney, bemoaning the agitation it would cause to men's minds and the instability it would bring to society, and cursing the low-grade self-seekers who might now presume to represent 'the people'. He lived out an exile that would endure, save for one brief interval, until his death in 1872.

Celebrated fiction writers have intuitively grasped the dramatic and often tragic qualities of the vindictively driven character – Ahab in *Moby Dick*, Heathcliff in *Wuthering Heights*, Raskolnikov in *Crime and Punishment* to name but a few. Wentworth, in this vein, was one of the great dramatic characters in Australia's past. He was destined to play the lead in hammering out the nation's political foundations yet to fail in his own quest for power in government and honour in his own land. ◼

'God alone knows what terrible things are coming to them, but whatever they are they will meet them as they have met everything in the past. These bad men, these ruffians, who will make the life of Australian magistrates busy when they return with outrages upon all known municipal byelaws and other restrictions upon the free life – they are of the staff of heroes and are the most important thing on earth at this blessed moment.'

Will Dyson on the Australian soldiers after Villers-Bretonneux

the AIF in 1918

ROSS McMULLIN

It's April 1918, the climax of the greatest war there had ever been. After years of stalemate at the Western Front – the decisive arena, despite attempts to circumvent the deadlock with campaigns elsewhere, including Gallipoli – there is substantial movement at last.

But for Australia's soldiers, the AIF, this news is disconcerting. The British have been driven back up to forty miles in the Somme sector; Amiens and the Channel Ports, strategically critical, look vulnerable. After years of ghastly casualties that will blight a generation, a grim possibility looms: Britain and its allies might well lose the war.

AIF units are rushed to the rescue. The spirit of these Australians is striking. The demoralised disarray they encounter doesn't deter them. They are pleased to have a different role after being directed to make a series of costly and mostly ill-conceived attacks since 1915. After all, stopping the Germans from rampaging across Europe is precisely why many Australians enlisted in the first place.

Distressed Frenchwomen, vacating homes threatened by the German advance, are thrilled when the Australians arrive and distribute nonchalant reassurance: *'Fini retreat madame, beaucoup Australiens ici.'* (Has there ever been a more splendid Australian affirmation?) Confident that the Australians will resist the Germans, many civilians retrace their steps and reoccupy their homes amid rapturous cries of 'Vive l'Australie!'

The advent of the AIF proves significant. Although the German advance is beginning to overextend, the Australians' resolve and resourcefulness are influential – and in a nationally distinctive way. Non-Australian observers notice this and acclaim it. Australia's soldiers, bolstering resistance in vulnerable sectors, are aware they are different and aware they are making a difference. With their competence and confidence conspicuous, their contribution inspires esteem. Brigadier-General Harold 'Pompey' Elliott, Australia's most famous fighting general, has seen plenty of war – the landing at Gallipoli, the cauldron of Lone Pine, the catastrophe near Fromelles. Now he writes in April 1918 that he 'was never so proud of being an Australian'.

Six days later, with the sense of crisis still acute, the Germans capture the tactically vital town of Villers-Bretonneux overlooking Amiens. Concern about this development reaches the highest levels. Pompey Elliott's brigade and another Australian brigade are directed to recapture the town. It's a complex operation in the dark with minimal artillery support, but this stunningly successful counter-attack is hailed as the most brilliant feat of the war. Amiens is under threat no longer.

Later in 1918 some AIF exploits surpass even Villers-Bretonneux. In a transformation following the failure of the German onslaught, the Australians become prominent in a sweeping advance to eventual victory. This starts, for the AIF, on 4 July at Hamel. The new Australian Corps commander, Lieutenant-General John Monash, orchestrates an attack that proceeds like clockwork with impressive tactical sophistication and tank–infantry cooperation. Hamel becomes the precursor to an ambitious assault spearheaded by Australians and Canadians. On 8 August the AIF advances seven miles in seven hours, capturing 7,925 prisoners and 173 guns, despite being hampered by the inability of a British corps alongside to accomplish its main task, the capture of Chipilly. Remarkably, an enterprising AIF patrol of two sergeants and four privates achieves the following night what the British corps could not: the intrepid half dozen Australians, with British infantry following up behind, drive the Germans out of Chipilly.

Further battles follow to consolidate the ascendancy gained on 8 August. Fighting is still fierce. Casualties keep accumulating. But Monash can see a war-winning opportunity – and wants to deny the enemy respite. More Australian victories drive the Germans back. Among an impressive field of notable feats, the AIF's capture of Mont St Quentin is astonishing.

And their battlefield sway increases as their battalion strength decreases. Dwindling reinforcements have already led to the disbandment of three battalions; others are to follow. Years of war have weakened other combatants' forces too, but not the Americans whose involvement has been brief.

American infantry, keen but green, join the Australians in a leapfrog operation to capture the formidable Hindenburg Line. On 29 September, Pompey Elliott is dismayed to discover that his brigade, on its way forward with other AIF formations to extend the Americans' initial advance, is suffering casualties because the Americans have not properly consolidated at the first objective. Elliott sorts out the failings of the American general, and his brigade completes the Americans' task as well as its own.

Elsewhere the state of affairs is similar. AIF photographer George Wilkins finds himself in a trench with Americans who are unaware they are being bombed by *nearby* Germans. Wilkins alerts them, grabs someone's rifle, and helps to retrieve the situation with such inspiring effectiveness that he is awarded a second distinction, a Bar to his Military Cross. These and other events confirm that the Americans' reliance on the AIF in 1918 could hardly be more unlike the relationship between the two nations familiar to later generations.

Since March 1918 the AIF has captured more than twenty per cent of the prisoners, guns and territory secured by the British though comprising less than ten per cent of the overall British force. What Australia's soldiers have accomplished in these momentous months – in both defence and attack – prompts the conclusion that Australians have influenced the destiny of the world in 1918 more than Australians have done in any other year.

Commemorating what happened at Gallipoli in 1915 is understandable. Remembering what happened at the Western Front in 1918 is fundamental. ∎

lake mungo

TIM MURRAY

I first visited the Willandra Lakes over twenty years ago, driving from Mildura through what seemed to be endless low scrub and grasslands, flat and grey-green in the white light of summer. Mungo, especially the Walls of China, was a revelation. In the late afternoon the fantastic shapes and colours of this complex erosion landscape came alive. Scattered across the dunes, in the shadows cast by gullies and pedestals of fine sand, were abundant stone tools, animal bones and shells – the raw materials for writing the human history of the place.

In 1981 the fifth session of the World Heritage Committee meeting in Paris inscribed the Willandra Lakes region of New South Wales on the World Heritage List, making it among the first three Australian sites to be recognised (the other two being Kakadu National Park and the Great Barrier Reef). The criteria for selection on the list are stringent, the most important being that the place has to be of 'outstanding universal value', and the Willandra Lakes region qualified because of the extraordinary testimony to the human and environmental history of Australia that lies preserved in its archaeology and geomorphology. The listing of the Willandra Lakes was the culmination of many years of survey and excavation that followed the initial reconnaissance by geomorphologist Jim Bowler in 1967. Remarkably, Bowler has continued his close association with Mungo and its people for forty years, and his work has been absolutely fundamental in developing our understanding of the area, and in establishing a working relationship with traditional owners to support continuing research there.

The Willandra Lakes region – and Mungo in particular – is a place of superlatives. Its physical landscape contains the longest and most complete record of landscape and climate change in Australia. Its archaeological record comprises the longest continuous history of human occupation, from the beginning of settlement some 45,000 years ago to the present. At Mungo, we have the oldest securely dated archaeological traces in the continent, and the impacts of European settlement on the landscape of the region are also clearly visible. Mungo is a place where we can learn much about the interactions between human beings and the environment throughout the history of Australia. But while the region is a natural and cultural archive of priceless importance, Mungo is also a place very much in the present for the three indigenous communities who are its traditional owners, and who now jointly manage the Mungo National Park that lies at the core of the World Heritage Area.

The Willandra Lakes are an interconnected string of dry lake basins in the far south-west of New South Wales, lying near the junction of the Murray, Darling, Lachlan and Murrumbidgee rivers. Long ago the region was a massive floodplain fed by melt from the snow and ice of the south-eastern highlands. It was, and continues to be, a very active physical landscape that reflects changing climatic conditions in the south-east of Australia over the last 20 million years. The thirteen lakes cover an area of approximately 4,000 square kilometres, with the most significant being Mulurulu, Garnpung, Leaghur, Mungo and Arumpo, and were formed some 400,000 years ago when drier conditions led to the formation of dune fields that cut off the Willandra Creek.

Bowler has recognised five main horizons and each represents a 'chapter' in the history of the regional landscape, providing the 'chronological spine' of the Mungo story. Characteristically, the narrative rests on the consequences of water – or lack of it – over many millennia. Indeed, the spectacular discoveries of ancient human remains (Mungo Lady, a cremated skeleton some 42,000 to 38,000 years old and Mungo Man, a skeleton dating to the same period that was covered in ochre) were made in the crescent-shaped dunes of sand and clay, called lunettes, which lie in an east–west orientation on the north-east margins of each of the lakes. The formation, stabilisation and erosion of these dunes were a direct response to water levels in the lakes and the strength and direction of the prevailing winds.

The lowest unit, the Gol Gol, dates to a period over 100,000 years ago. Then there is the Mungo unit, dating from about 55,000 to about 17,000 years ago, a time of fluctuating lake levels, abundant resources and much evidence of human activity. Life must have been good at times of high lake levels, with freshwater fish and shellfish complementing a diet made up of wild foods, which probably included now-extinct megafauna such as the giant short-faced kangaroo *(Procoptodon goliah)*. Yet, even during the dryer phases, human habitation of the area continued with adaptations being made to a drastically changing environment, such as the grinding of wild grass seeds to produce flour. Above this is the Zanci unit that reflects a gradual drying up of the system and a return to dune formation due to wind action. Aboriginal people continued their occupation of the area for the next 17,000 years before European settlement, but focused their activities away from the dunes.

Mungo has been a place of landmark archaeological discoveries: Mungo Lady is the oldest ritual cremation in the world, and the stone tools found in the Mungo unit helped define the Australian core tool and scraper tradition. Nonetheless, our understanding of the rich archaeological record of the region is still rudimentary as surprisingly little research has been undertaken since the 1970s. Recently this has changed as the traditional owners have sought to closely collaborate with research scientists so that such fragile ancient riches can be documented and better managed. The return of the remains of Mungo Lady to the control of the traditional owners, and the recent discovery of human footprints made over 20,000 years ago, are signs of a positive future for the past of this remarkable place. ■

AN' THERE I TOLD 'ER 'OW I'D DONE ME DASH

the sentimental bloke

JULIE RIGG

Louis Stone's novel *Jonah*, published in 1911, was the first Australian novel to explore the culture of the urban working class. While the bush balladeers held sway in the popular press, Stone drew on his observations of Sydney's gangs, or 'pushes', to fashion the lives of two push graduates: Jonah, who went on to become a ruthless businessman, and his mate, Chook, who married red-haired Pinky and settled for a life of domestic bliss.

It wasn't a popular book: Jonah himself was a figure of tragedy. But when, four years later, C.J. Dennis, a jobbing journalist from Melbourne, persuaded George Robertson to publish a book based on some of his *Bulletin* verses, *The Songs of the Sentimental Bloke* struck a chord. Australian readers cherished this story of a hard-drinking, brawling larrikin tamed by love. They enjoyed the way it rhymed and relished the vernacular, and its jibes against authority and middle-class pretension. In some editions, the book was published with a glossary to enable genteel readers to interpret the lingo.

My father quoted it often. 'Er name's Doreen,' he would say, sighing theatrically when my mum appeared, dolled up for some occasion. 'Cor, what a peach.' Or if one of us was acting up, he would interject, 'She grabs a pocket knife to end 'er cares! "Peanuts or lollies," sez the boy upstairs.'

C.J. Dennis set *The Bloke* in unspecified parts of Melbourne. When Raymond Longford, a stage actor turned screen director, took on the job of making a film version, he made some crucial decisions. Longford moved the film production to Woolloomooloo in Sydney, a port suburb equally renowned for its pushes and razor gangs. His film shows the cramped parlours, worn front steps and picket fences of the 'Loo, and its street life, pub doorways, drays pulling fruit and vegetables, and barrels of beer.

He also took pains with casting. Arthur Tauchert, who plays the Bloke, had been a labourer who turned to vaudeville. Actually of German origin, he had a broad Mick face, gap teeth and a suit coat straining at its buttons. His mate, Ginger Mick, is a whippet-like Woolloomooloo lair, all bravado and braces.

Lottie Lyell, the young Balmain-born actress who had become Longford's protégée, then lover and collaborator, played Doreen. In Dennis' verses, we see Doreen through the eyes of the besotted Bloke, and she is idealised, blue-eyed and golden-haired – a rather soppy picture of reforming womanhood.

Lyell's Doreen is in the tradition of the Chaplin waif, but with something more. With her long face and dark eyes under strong brows, she brought a spirit that fills out the role and gives Doreen a shrewd independence.

The scenes between Tauchert and Lyell in their courtship are touching. The way she snubs him when he first tries to chat her up. The look she gives him when he first declares his passion and tries to kiss her, lifting up her face in a grip which almost mashes her jaw. We can see alarm, decision to trust, and joy on her face in one swift moment.

One of the hallmarks of Raymond Longford's direction was its naturalism. Silent cinema had a language of gesture, partly derived from vaudeville, which was often overlarge. Longford, by contrast, let glances and movement within the scene convey mood as well as story. The inter-titles were spare. They kept the wit and spirit of Dennis' verse, while avoiding the archness and vernacular overkill.

In a sense, Longford and Lyell's triumph was to return the Bloke to his working-class origins, replacing the twee cupid imagery of Hal Gye's illustrations with imagery more closely anchored in Australian life.

A hit in Australia and New Zealand, the film foundered in America, where it was released as *The Story of a Tough Guy*, with American gangsterisms replacing Dennis's Australian slang. Ironically though, eighty years later a copy of the American version enabled the Australian Screen and Sound Archive to restore Longford's version.

Lottie Lyell died in 1925, of tuberculosis. She was just 35. Her achievements as Australia's first great silent-film star overshadowed her work as a film-maker, editor and screenwriter, in partnership with Longford.

Longford fought many battles, unsuccessfully, to persuade Australian governments to support and protect Australian cinema against the tide of American talkies, and the practices of the US-led cinema 'combine'. By the 1950s he was working as a nightwatchman on the Sydney wharves. He died in 1959.

The Bloke was the first in a succession of larrikin figures that haunt Australian popular culture. From Ginger Meggs to Paul Hogan and Strop, from Breaker Morant to Kenny the Portaloo Philosopher, the larrikin keeps reappearing in most generations to give the finger to authority and undermine pretension. He is a leveller, and sometimes anti-intellectual, but he's a brawler with a soft heart.

Maybe he stands for the Australian values at their kindly best. Or maybe he makes us all feel safer on the streets. ∎

nick cave

TONY DAVIS

From the first, when that thudding bass scuds into a beat-backed, thoroughly malevolent chorus chanting the name Deanna, the ears can't help but prick up.

The lead singer, a gun-toting piece of white trash surrounded by charred Christmas trees and 'Ku Klux furniture', sounds like a homicidal incarnation of Buddy Holly as his crazed, hiccupping vocal announces he isn't down here for love or money but 'down here for your soul'.

A contrast: the dragging, almost apologetic beat and haunting organ of 'Brompton Oratory'. The listener is soon in an old English church, where a tormented lover is wishing aloud that he – like the surrounding apostles – were made of stone, so he didn't have to look at a beauty impossible to endure.

That the two songs are the work of the same person is surprising, more so that he is a former private schoolboy from regional Victoria.

The catalogue of Nick Cave – singer, lyricist, composer, writer, provocateur – is peopled with gothic misfits. There's the man tormented by his shadow who eventually hunts it down and the carney who walks out on the sideshow freaks, leaving them to bury his horse as a biblical flood consumes the 'eaten earth'.

There are characters with the devil constantly peering over their shoulder, guiding them inevitably towards murder then the gallows. Jilted lovers, beggars, fringe-dwellers. One man hides a red right hand in his dusty black coat, another contemplates suicide as grief comes riding up the River Thames and the ancient iron bridge groans under the weight of people returning to their failures and boredoms.

The musical landscapes range from sweeping piano-driven ballads, wild blues, gospel, angular arthouse rock and, just occasionally, almost flawless three-minute pop songs. In recent years Cave's team of grotesques has been joined and eventually captained by a character who might be the man behind the masks: a contemplative, highly religious troubadour.

In the Martin Scorsese film *No Direction Home*, Bob Dylan stated: 'An artist has got to be careful to never arrive at a place where he thinks he's at somewhere. You always have to realise that you're constantly in a state of becoming.'

Few musicians have embraced such a philosophy as strongly as Cave. Even fewer have achieved international success over three decades without deteriorating into a nostalgia act or velcroing themselves to a style or niche.

Although never playing up his national origins, Cave has underlined his work with dark and unmistakably irreverent Australian humour. Other musicians may celebrate their 50th year by pretending to be 25, Cave recorded the *No Pussy Blues*. Almost as raucous as anything in his catalogue, it decries that increasing age and ugliness has eroded his appeal to groupies ('I read her Eliot, I read her Yeats, I tried my best to stay up late . . . but still, she just never wanted to.')

Cave started out in the late 1970s with short pop songs – as quirky as they were catchy – then abandoned them almost immediately as some sort of embarrassing teenage mistake. At first it was in favour of longer, darker songs, then suddenly things became very black indeed. As Cave faced the sudden death of his father and a growing problem with alcohol then heroin, the poppy Boys Next Door became the acerbic, vengeful Birthday Party.

Concerts were a metaphorical – and, occasionally, physical – attack on the audience. Cave had only contempt for hopeful punters who called for the 'old' songs (which is to say ones from just one or two years earlier). That was then. Now was the time for musical Dadaism.

Much as they often tried, Cave and his cohorts couldn't completely bury their musicality. The Birthday Party weren't *avant garde* merely because they couldn't do *garde*. Even in an unsettling ode to a 'Zoo Music Girl', in which Cave screams for the right to 'die beneath her fists', there were solid pop sensibilities.

Tentative international success came with the Birthday Party in the early 1980s. As the imitators moved in, or perhaps as the listeners thought they had his measure, Cave was off again, lost in a mix of biblical and Deep South imagery, set to gospel-tinged proto-rock and outcast blues (such as 'Deanna', from 1988).

With new personnel and a new name – it was now Nick Cave and the Bad Seeds – they found a more stable platform in Cave's increasingly literary lyrics and made a slow drift back to a more mainstream sound.

Moving on was a habit Cave would not relinquish. *The Boatman's Call*, an album of ballads from 1997, had soaring melodies and moving, highly personal lyrics. Yet he chose to end it all with the profanity-laden and almost tune-free 'Green Eyes'. One suspects Cave will forever be the unreliable narrator – the one who will not be pigeon-holed, much less caught out with an unqualified commercial success. Indeed the one who, when belatedly and perhaps begrudgingly given a 'place' in the Australian music industry's ARIA Hall of Fame in 2007, would spend his acceptance speech personally 'inducting' other people he thought had been overlooked.

Cave's body of work is immense and varied, with more than a dozen albums with the Bad Seeds alone. His songs have been covered by Metallica and Johnny Cash. There is a surprisingly good novel, *And the Ass Saw the Angel*, plus screenplays and soundtracks. There have been some acting roles too, though no one has been brave enough to argue the case for greatness there.

It is for contemporary music Cave will be primarily judged, and with this art form so much depends on where you were at what time, and what you were looking for. No one can be convinced Cave is a 'great' if they don't find it in the words or music, any more than the true believers could be swayed by arguments to the contrary, no matter how well-formed.

It says enough that, as a songwriter and performer, Cave is loved and despised, extolled and bitterly derided. In his milieu, that's as much as anyone could possibly hope to achieve. ∎

thin air: the michael groom story

LINCOLN HALL

At the summit of Mount Everest the low air density reduces the available oxygen to thirty per cent of the quantity we enjoy at sea level. 'Thin air' is how climbers refer to the sparsely oxygenated air, and mountaineer Michael Groom thrives on it. He was drawn to it even before he knew it existed.

When he was six years old, Michael stood in front of his class at Beechmont Public School in south-east Queensland and told everyone that when he grew up he would climb Mount Everest. There had been only five successful Everest expeditions at that time, so it was not surprising that his classmates laughed at his ambition.

For the next fifteen years Michael Groom kept his dream to himself. At 21 he took the first steps on the long path to the summit of Everest. He learnt the essential skills of mountaineering in New Zealand, one of the best training grounds for any climber. In 1987, on his fourth Himalayan expedition, Michael and his climbing partner, John Coulton, made the first Australian ascent of Kanchenjunga. Not only was it the world's third-highest peak but it was also one of the most challenging. Michael and John had climbed as a team of two, without Sherpa support or supplementary oxygen, which was an amazing achievement.

Unfortunately, their descent was a disaster almost from the outset. Darkness fell with the two men separated high on the mountain. Two days later their paths crossed and they staggered down to Base Camp together. Both suffered temporary blindness and frostbite that left permanent damage. In Michael's case, he was unable to walk. The frostbite had taken not only all his toes but thirty per cent of both of his feet as well.

After three weeks in hospital in Brisbane and months of follow-up visits, he was advised to buy a wheelchair and find a desk job. Instead, he vowed to get on his own two feet again – or what was left of them. Michael states that learning to walk was the hardest challenge he has had to face in a life full of challenges.

Eighteen months after the ordeal on Kanchenjunga, Michael was back in the Everest region to climb the dramatic peak of Ama Dablam, a mountain two kilometres lower than Everest. The climbing was not too difficult but his feet were very tender, and the cold only added to the pain. Nevertheless, he took the opportunity of the isolation to kick his eighteen-month addiction to painkillers. He simply brought too few of the drugs to see him through the expedition. He decided that getting 'clean' in the thin cold air of the Himalaya was the best way to go – a true case of cold turkey.

On his return to Queensland, he was invited to join an expedition to Cho Oyu, the sixth-highest mountain in the world. He expected the mountain to be beyond his capabilities, but he turned out to be the only team member to reach the summit. Again, he rejected oxygen equipment.

Michael's success on Cho Oyu gave him his life back. Everest was only 550 metres higher, and he believed his dream was within his reach. On his first attempt an avalanche swept him 900 metres down the steep icy Lhotse face, but a broken nose and a few cracked ribs were his only injuries. In 1993 he stood on the summit of Mount Everest, his life-long goal achieved, without supplementary oxygen. The following year he climbed K2, the world's second-highest mountain. Despite its nondescript name, it is considered to be the hardest of the world's giant peaks, as well as one the most dangerous. But it was in 1996, on his second climb of Everest, that he faced his most confronting dangers. He reached the summit as a guide during the infamous storm that killed eight people, the deadliest storm in Everest's history. More people would have died had it not been for Michael's efforts during the night-time blizzard at 8000 metres.

When Michael reached the summit of K2, he had climbed the three highest mountains in the world, all without oxygen, but he wasn't ready to leave the thin air of the high Himalaya. He set himself the new target of climbing the five highest peaks. The two remaining mountains were Lhotse, which he went on to climb in 1995, and Makalu. On 16 May 1999, Michael stood on the summit of Makalu, his quest at an end, with an achievement matched only by a handful of others.

Michael never really speaks of Cho Oyu, which he climbed in 1990, except in the context of it giving him the confidence to tackle Everest. He puts the Big Five peaks in a different dimension of effort and danger. On those five mountains, climbers have the choice of camping above 8000 metres, an altitude known as the Death Zone, or of enduring a very long and cold summit day from a lower, safer camp. Only very strong climbers can manage the latter option, and Michael Groom is in that rare company. Without oxygen, it is much harder to climb fast, stay warm and avoid deadly altitude sickness, but Michael chooses that path. He prefers the purity of the process and the emptiness of the thin cold air. ■

Speedo. The best thing next to a suntan.

the speedo

MARGOT RILEY

September 2007, Sydney: 1010 bikini-clad women nestle into the sand at Bondi Beach and pose for the world's largest ever swimsuit photoshoot, setting a new world record and prompting the Australian-born *Guinness Book of World Records* adjudicator to say, 'Any record involving sun, sand and surf should be held in this country.'

Arriving in Sydney from Scotland in 1910, Alexander MacRae must also have recognised the near-religious cultural significance of swimming and surfing to a population who enjoyed easy access to the water and the ideal climate for aquatic leisure. Soon after establishing the MacRae Knitting Mill as an underwear manufactory in 1914, he quickly expanded his operations to include swimwear.

National water prowess had already placed Australia at the centre of the world aquatic sports arena. Fred Lane became the country's first Olympic gold-medal swimmer at the 1900 Paris Games, with Sarah 'Fanny' Durack becoming Australia's first female gold medallist in 1912. Andrew 'Boy' Charlton, a 16-year-old from Manly, astounded spectators at the 1924 NSW State Championships when he beat visiting reigning world champion Arne Borg. Charlton went on to break Borg's 1500m world record, winning gold at the 1924 Paris Games.

In the late 1920s, the MacRae Knitting Mill developed a figure-hugging, one-piece cotton knit jersey swimming costume with a 'racer back'. This revolutionary design bared the upper arms and shoulders like a singlet, permitting greater freedom of movement. Renaming the company Speedo Knitting Mills in 1928, after their slogan 'Speedo-on in your Speedos', the racing suit went into production in 1929. MacRae swiftly planted the new brand name at the forefront of competitive swimming through celebrity endorsement, using a publicity photograph of Arne Borg wearing the racer back costume, taken during his 1927 Australian tour.

The Speedo name still encapsulates the company's goal to develop and utilise the latest in performance-enhancing design and technological innovation to give athletes the edge on the clock. The main function of a racing swimsuit is to reduce a swimmer's drag in the water. Over the last century, the pendulum has swung from 'neck-to-knee' and back again in the quest for a streamlined swimsuit that hugs the body, minimising friction and water retention. The evolution from wool to silk and cotton, and from nylon to lycra, has culminated in the development of the world's first 'fast' swimwear fabrics.

Speedo launched its revolutionary full-length 'Fastskin' swimsuit just in time for the 2000 Sydney Olympics. Featuring silicon-printed textures inspired by the unique denticular (tooth-shaped) patterns on shark skin, the shape-hugging suit cuts through water with minimum drag and turbulence.

In complete contrast to this full-length, high-performance swimsuit, Speedo also invented the male 'bikini'. Speedo swim briefs, like underwear briefs, feature a 'V-shape' front and solid, form-fitting coverage on the back. Made of a nylon and lycra/spandex composite, they are typically worn low on the hips, secured by a cord drawstring tie with thin elasticised banding at the upper thighs. Colloquially known as 'budgie smugglers', the modern Speedo swim brief has eleven slang terms listed in the Macquarie dictionary, marking the iconic status of this quintessentially Australian invention. It's also indicative of how our culture works – using wicked euphemisms and cutting tall poppies down to size.

The swim brief was actually invented for *fashion*, not speed. A Manly-born designer, Peter Travis, was hired by Speedo in the early 1960s to create their first international men's leisurewear range. Travis decided to make something the world didn't have – a swimsuit that looked good, fitted well and was comfortable to wear. Up until this time, men's swimwear had been available in three main styles: the traditional unitard with shoulder straps, boxer-style swim shorts and form-fitting, waist-high trunks with a built-in front modesty panel known as a half-skirt. Anticipating the sexual revolution, Travis's 1961 design trimmed the swim trunk sides down from the standard fifteen inches to a relatively skimpy eight inches.

Gloria Smythe, sole designer at Speedo from 1962 to 1991, made innovations in the company's quest for speed through her research into garment hydrodynamics (movement through water). Smythe also added pattern and colour to Olympic team swimwear, combining fashion and competitive swimming for the first time. In 1964, she removed the half-skirts from the men's suits and kitted out the Australian Olympic team in green-and-gold striped togs. Panelled suits came next, then prints, and as Speedos' fashion stakes went up, their medal tally also increased. Between the 1968 and 1976 Games practically every gold-medallist swimmer wore Speedos. Necklines dropped, hiplines rose and the width of the men's brief was gradually whittled down, an inch at time, to a mere two inches by 1972 – a look that quickly became an Australian icon and just as swiftly went worldwide, transforming men's swimwear forever.

Australians have always made icons of things that divert them from hard times. The beach is our haven of egalitarianism and the natural habitat of the surf lifesaver, the surfer and the sunbather. All three icons are an embodiment of modern Australia: young, free and far removed from the beleaguered convict, the squatter and the digger. Bronzed Aussies, standing at the edge of a sparkling blue ocean clad only in their 'cossies' – a global image of Australia today – sand, surf and skimpy Speedos, the sartorial emblem of our long hot summers. ■

Here comes summer !

EQUATOR/SAILCLOTH Cotton Mesh "Swim-Jacket". Trimmed with BRI-NYLON. SM-XOS, **49/11.** Cotton Sailcloth "Ben Buckler" short. Stretch BRI-NYLON side panel. 30"-40", **39/11.** Also available for boys. 26"-32", **35/-.**

ACAPULCA Cotton print "Cabana" top. SM-XOS, **55/-.** Cotton print "Boxer" short. 30"-40", **39/11.** Boys' styles also available.

NARRABEEN/LANIAKEA Striped cotton shirt, SM-XOS, **29/11.** Also available for boys, 28"-34", **25/-.** Woven cotton "Surfari" short. Stretch BRI-NYLON leg gusset, wax pocket. 28"-36", **47/6.**

STRIPED JETSTREAM Girls' BRI-NYLON suit, ¼ skirt. 24"-28", **37/6.** 30"-34"L, 36"-38", **59/6.**

SPEEDO'S *ready !*

SPEEDO

**READY FOR YOU NOW
ALL OVER AUSTRALIA**

(YOU'LL FIND SPEEDO AT EVERY GOOD STORE).

patrick white

ELIZABETH WEBBY

Patrick White's relationship with Australia and Australians was always
problematic. As a scion of the squattocracy, born and largely educated in England,
White was certainly not a typical Australian. But nor was he content to follow
the path mapped out for him: he loved the Australian landscape but not his two
years working on the land. The literary career he chose initially meant living in
London as an expatriate. But in 1946, after fourteen years away, White returned
to Australia. He told an English friend, 'I had not realised how Australian I am
underneath until I came back and saw it and smelled it again.' And in 'The
Prodigal Son', written in 1958 in response to a piece by expatriate poet Alister
Kershaw, White spoke of the rewards of returning home, of new insights, of the
possibility of 'helping to people a barely inhabited country with a race possessed
of understanding'.

    In *The Tree of Man* and *Voss,* the novels written in the ten years after his
return, White took on the two classic stories of Australian settlement: pioneering
and exploration. In both, however, he was determined to work against prevailing
stereotypes as well as literary styles, not only rejecting the 'journalistic realism'
of earlier historical sagas but the heroic, celebratory mode. Stan Parker of *The
Tree of Man* is not a member of the squattocracy but a small farmer; while he
struggles against such typically Australian crises as fire and flood, his biggest
challenges come from his relationships with his wife and children. And his

greatest achievement is a spiritual one: the realisation that even the ugliest and most abject aspects of life have a meaning. Voss, in contrast, who wills himself to be a hero, is humbled by the very things he had hoped to conquer: the land and its indigenous inhabitants. His actual journey of exploration is paralleled by the imaginative one of Laura Trevelyan, whom he meets briefly in Sydney. Again White's stress is on the spiritual journeys and discoveries of his characters rather than their material ones.

After these rewritings of Australian history, White turned to the contemporary scene, enlarging his satirical representations of Australian complacency, materialism and xenophobia. *Riders in the Chariot* was the first of several works to be set in 'Sarsaparilla', otherwise Castle Hill on Sydney's north-west outskirts, where White and his partner, Manoly Lascaris, had lived since 1948. Its four 'riders' are all, as White believed himself to be, outcasts from the mainstream: a Jewish refugee; an eccentric spinster; a working-class mother; an Aboriginal artist. Although written nearly fifty years ago, the novel seems all too contemporary in its representations of intolerance of difference, drunken larrikinism that easily tips over into violence and the abuse suffered by members of the Stolen Generation. *The Solid Mandala,* also set in Sarsaparilla, again questions pragmatic materialism in its contrast between the sterile, would-be intellectual Waldo and his supposedly dim-witted brother, Arthur, who has an intuitive love of life.

White's move from Castle Hill to Centennial Park in Sydney's east marked the end of his Sarsaparilla period. Apart from *A Fringe of Leaves,* published in 1976 but begun in 1961, an historical novel based on the story of Eliza Fraser, his later work has a more strongly personal focus. *The Vivisector* traces the life of an Australian painter while being at the same time a portrait of 'wet, boiling, superficial, brash, beautiful, ugly Sydney'. As its title suggests, a major concern is how great art is achieved at the expense of those intimately involved with the artist. *The Eye of the Storm* demonstrates this through its depiction of a central character based on White's mother, with whom he always had a difficult relationship. (His decision to stay in Australia after the war was partly determined by her move to London.) His final major novel, *The Twyborn Affair*, however, ends with a mother's acceptance of her son's transformation into a woman. Here, revisiting some of the scenes of his first three novels, *Happy Valley*, *The Living and the Dead* and *The Aunt's Story*, White depicted a central character who switches between male and female roles in the way White himself had been able to do in his fiction. Its success prompted him to write a frank and controversial autobiography, *Flaws in the Glass.*

If White's later novels moved away from the more obviously national themes of his middle period, he himself was much more in the public eye after 1973, when he became the first Australian to win the Nobel Prize for Literature. Although a reluctant public speaker, he joined in many community and political campaigns, especially those opposing the nuclear industry he saw as the greatest threat to life on earth. In 1988 he ended what was to be his last public address still hoping that 'the path of humility and humanity' might allow Australia to develop 'a civilisation worthy of the name'. ■

the sentimental nation

JOHN HIRST

A sentimental attachment to the continent and its people, as a nation-in-waiting, long preceded the formalities in Sydney's Centennial Park on 1 January 1901.

The Australian coat-of-arms, formally adopted in 1912, derived from folk art. For decades the kangaroo and emu had been facing each other on mugs, shields, certificates, tokens, embroidery, the plates hung around the necks of Aboriginal 'kings', the pediments of buildings and tags to mark the registration of dogs. There was no doubt about which were the emblematic animals, but their stance varied according to the artist. They were more frisky than formal, and frequently they had their backs to the central shield, with their necks twisting and turning so that they might look at each other, as if the nation was to be bound together by a riveting glance. The oldest unofficial coat-of-arms, held by the Mitchell Library, is painted in oils on a wood panel and has been dated to the early 1820s.

These amateurs in the college of heralds were centralists, not federalists. The official coat-of-arms has the emblems of the six states on its central shield, which makes it a crowded object; the amateurs had the shield divided into four parts usually carrying representations of the golden fleece, a wheatsheaf, a ship and a miner's pick and shovel. The latter appear after the gold rushes of the 1850s, replacing a ship's anchor and harpoon.

From the beginning the motto across the bottom was 'Advance Australia' and at the top were the rays of the rising sun. With its convict origins Australia had to hope that the future would give it the glories that other nations could boast in their past. 'Advance' was dropped from the official coat-of-arms, but in their national anthem Australians are still looking for the advance of their nation. 'Advance Australia Fair' also long predates the formal nation, being composed by Peter McCormick in 1878. It was one of hundreds of national poems and songs, mostly dreadfully amateurish and without the primitive vigour of the coats-of-arms. By 1878 the sentiments surrounding the coming nation were already so well established that McCormick had to do no more than hint at them. The most puzzling line to modern Australians, 'our land is girt by sea', refers to God designating a whole continent for nationhood, which gave it only natural borders and a place apart from the corruptions of the world.

A continent for a nation was a magnificent offering, the gift of the British Empire, which to its denizens was acting as proxy for God. When Matthew Flinders sailed round the continent from 1802 to 1803, British settlement extended no more than a day's horse ride from Sydney Cove. When Governor Lachlan Macquarie successfully urged that 'Australia', which Flinders coined, become the official name, settlement had begun in Van Diemen's Land, but 95 per cent of the continent remained in Aboriginal hands. At this stage New South Wales was the only Australian colony, occupying the eastern half of the continent, and the tendency of its people to mistake it for Australia began. When Western Australia was founded in 1829, Britain completed its claim to the continent, which it protected from the sea rather than by systematically settling its lands. When the French Ambassador in London in the 1850s asked the Colonial Office how much of Australia the British claimed, he was told 'the whole'.

But what did God intend by creating Bass Strait? In the nineteenth century 'Australia' did not include Tasmania, but the federal plans of the nationalists on the continent always included Tasmania, which was particularly anxious to join the union. Briefly around 1890 the federation looked as if it might include New Zealand and even islands in the Pacific, for which there was another name waiting – Australasia – but with Tasmania finally as the only exception to continental unity 'Australia' was stretched to accommodate it.

In 1901 a competition was held for a design of an Australian flag. Five winners were declared who had each submitted a similar design. This convergence was not surprising since the elements of the flag, the Union Jack in the top left corner and the Southern Cross in the fly, had long been in use on colonial flags and banners. Except for the six-pointed star under the Union Jack, the winning flag was an exact replica of the flag created by the Anti-Transportation League in the 1850s, which can still be seen in the Launceston Museum.

Other nations have had to develop their symbols – coat-of-arms, anthem, flag, even their name – after they were formed or they emerged in the process of nation-making. Australia's symbols were well established long before the move to federation began. So why is federation commonly thought of as a pragmatic business deal with little or no national sentiment? – because an unromantic scepticism has become the national style. ∎

the sheep's back

JOHN EDWARDS

It was only eleven years after the First Fleet arrived at Sydney Cove that Captain
John Macarthur of the New South Wales Corps obtained three merino rams and
five merino ewes from the Cape of Good Hope to breed with his inferior flock of
hair-bearing stock. The experiment was an astonishing success, producing sheep
with dense, fine wool suitable for the looms of England. By 1801, only 13 years
after the settlement, Macarthur had 2000 sheep in his flock alone. By 1813 there
were 50,000 sheep in the colony, and pastoralists had run out of land around
Sydney. When the Blue Mountains were crossed that same year, the wool growers
followed. By 1821 the colony had nearly 300,000 sheep in the national flock, and
the long pastoral boom was building.

Australian wool arrived just in time for the British textile industry.
Hitherto the dominant fibre, wool lost its pre-eminence to cotton around the
time the First Fleet anchored in Sydney Cove. Apart from cotton's greater ease
of manufacture into clothing, wool was constrained by available supply in the
United Kingdom and Europe. The development of the American cotton industry
offered a vast new supply to English fabric makers, helping cotton overtake wool
as the United Kingdom's largest industry in the early nineteenth century. The
wool spinners responded to the competition by developing techniques such
as mechanical combing, to which the new Australian wool was well adapted.
Through the nineteenth century the United States and Australia became the

great suppliers to the British textile industry. Cotton accounted for two-thirds of US exports by the time of the Civil War; wool accounted for two-thirds of Australian exports through to the end of World War II.

Sheep grew and reproduced quickly, and Australia at first accounted for such a small share of the London market for wool that all the production was readily sold. In 1835 it was plausibly estimated that a new pastoralist could invest less than £3000 to achieve a value of well over £9000 five years later, and in the meantime achieve an interest rate on the investment of just over seven per cent. By 1891, just before the long expansion of the industry was checked by the long slump of that decade, the Australian flock had reached over 106 million – considerably bigger than it would be a hundred years later. They produced 641 million pounds of wool, worth just short of £21,000,000. Wool paid Australia's way in the world.

Rivalled only by gold, wool-growing was for over a century Australia's uniquely successful industry and its claim to political attention and capital in London. It was also the epicentre of political struggle in the young colonies. Pastoralists needed not only merino stock (and the tireless sheep dog), but also cheap land and cheap labour. For many decades the industry depended on free land selected beyond the existing boundaries of settlement, and held on permissive and revocable titles – where there was a legal title at all. Land rights became a major battleground between the pastoralist 'squatters', the colonial Governor and the home government in London. In the early decades of European settlement, pastoralists were always the first to move beyond the existing boundaries of settlement – with or without permission. Their claim to cheap, abundant land brought them into conflict, not only with the English colonial authorities, but also with city folk and with farmers. For labour, they sought first the assignment of convicts and, when transportation to New South Wales was ended in 1840, immigrant shepherds from England or indentured labour from India and China. The English working-class of the cities and towns vehemently and successfully opposed the mass immigration of cheap labour, bringing them into conflict with the pastoralists. The pastoralists were often the first European settlers to interfere with Aboriginal land use, so that the outer perimeter of wool-growing was also the sharpest point of conflict with the native peoples. From the first few decades of settlement, the pastoralist interest had a strong voice, relentlessly pressing for cheap or free land, cheap or free labour, protection from Aborigines and bushrangers, and the elimination of duties on Australian wool imports to the United Kingdom.

Even in the middle of the twentieth century wool still accounted for nearly two-thirds of Australian exports and through the Country Party pastoralists remained an important political force. World War II, however, had stimulated the production of man-made fibres, and the vast expansion in oil demand provided the raw material for rapid growth in man-made textile output. After reaching new highs in the Korean War boom, wool prices began a long relative decline. Demand fell. The textile industries in the UK, the US and Europe collapsed under competition from emerging economies and man-made fibres. At the bidding of the pastoralists, the Country Party resisted the decline with new government price support and marketing programs, which had the effect of sustaining the industry beyond the size the declining global wool market would sustain.

Overproduction and the accumulation of vast stockpiles by the 1980s saw the value of wool production decline from $5.7 billion at the end of the decade to less than half that level at the end of the century. Wool accounted for just one-twentieth of Australian exports by 2007 – and it was difficult to recognise in the contemporary business the mighty force which, more than any other industry, shaped the Australian economy in the first 150 years after European settlement. Along the way, however, a smaller and more specialised industry had secured for itself a durable future. It was a producer of fine wools for high-quality garments such as men's suits. And it was also the supplier of wool to the fastest growing market in the world: China. ◾

the aussie backyard

HUGH STRETTON

Back in 1975 Ian Halkett earned his PhD flying low enough over Adelaide city and suburbs to photograph the details of a thousand household gardens. Five hundred householders answered a questionnaire about the design and uses of their outdoor space and what it contributed to their lives. Nine out of ten gardeners found the work itself as enjoyable as its effects. And my favourite among Halkett's discoveries: 'The back garden was used for recreation by more of the sampled households than was any other outdoor recreation facility.'

In 1956 I bought an 1899 two-storey four-bedroom house in walking distance of Adelaide University. Its front veranda was close to the street. Its kitchen and laundry doors opened onto a dusty clay backyard about forty feet square, under clothes lines and a walnut tree. On one side were a rusty rainwater tank and a gate to a sewer lane. On the other, a wire-netting henhouse lined the boundary fence. Across the back a stone-walled structure contained the WC, a woodshed, a horsebox and feed store, and shelter for a buggy.

It's versatile space. The horse and buggy and the hens and the old tank have long gone. Lemons, oranges, mint and parsley now grow in the yard. Roses climb the fences and flower gardens shape a lawn beneath clothes lines and a hammock. Children, dogs and their minders can all be happy here. Besides garden gear and bikes, the shed shelters the carpenter's bench and tools that have made most of our built-in bookshelves, bedroom wardrobes and drawers, kitchen cupboards and drawers and work surfaces.

House and garden are productive capital. What they enable parents and children to make and do and teach and learn, and to enjoy in family life and friendship, may often be more productive and diversely interesting than can be done in landless apartments and the mostly-paved, mostly-public spaces around them. Economists should not omit from 'domestic product' everything that house and garden equip and enable family members to produce – unpaid – for one another, including the experience and values that help to prepare children for adult life and paid work. The Hills Hoist and the backyard barbecue – Aussie icons – are *useful!*

So much for now. How might backyards fare in the various urban futures that we're warned to expect? Worldwide, the physical conditions of household life, especially in town, are famously threatened by the continuing growth of human numbers, the exhaustion or spoiling of resources on which their lives depend, and ill effects of likely climate changes. Where there is rainfall for crops, and some tanked or river water for stock and people, country life may survive those changes. In town, houses with backyards may be safer and more productive than landless flats or apartment towers. Roof water can be tanked and saved. Backyards may house poultry again, grow fruit and vegetables, shelter home trades in sheds. So the likely climatic and pollutant effects of tower apartment blocks and denser, higher housing overall don't seem good ideas to me. But if outdoor household space does need to be rationed, better lose the front garden than the backyard.

Our children and grandchildren might revive some old ideas in tandem with new ones. Replace our thirsty lawn and garden beds with the old hard clay backyard surface. Save its rainwater run-off for outdoor uses. Replace the walnut tree with a windmill generator and cover our roof with solar panels to reduce the need for other electric power. Drain the roof into bathroom and clothes-washing tanks. Only the clean water that we drink and cook with must all be bought from public or business suppliers.

Ian did not actually suggest restoring the horse and buggy. But I grew up with a brother and sister in a wooden house on a sand road, surrounded by ti-tree, half an hour on foot from schools, and an hour by tram and train from the city. We had ponies. Some local commercial traffic was still horse-drawn. A motor truck had only lately replaced the horse-and-cart whose crew exchanged empty dunny cans for our full ones every second Wednesday. (Burying that material beats flushing it with scarce water.) This part-sentimental, part-disgusting paragraph is not here for fun. Scientific attention to the destructive tendencies of our present ways of life, and our rates of economic growth and material exhaustion, needs to be matched by some mix of historical and imaginative thought about possible, tolerable – and even enjoyable – modes of daily human life and love and work that might be compatible with the austere new material conditions of our physical survival. And it may well be true that our rough Aussie past reveals the best evidence of our human capacities, especially for coping – painfully, patiently, sometimes inventively – with novel dangers and opportunities. ∎

the music of peter sculthorpe

ROBYN HOLMES

'For me', Peter Sculthorpe wrote in his 1999 autobiography *Sun Music: Journeys and Reflections from a Composer's Life,* 'Australia is the centre of the world.'

Peter Sculthorpe's driving vision has been to create music that is idiomatically and identifiably 'Australian'. This quest animates his music and largely accounts for his international recognition. He has shifted the musical axis from Europe towards his native land – its people, environment, mythology and history. Resident in Australia for most of his sixty-year career, Sculthorpe has become its most honoured and iconic living composer, the quintessential voice of Australian classical music.

The notion of 'Australian-ness' in music today barely causes a ripple with Australia's eye focused on its geographic setting in the Asia-Pacific. In artistic terms, Australian painters are known for their distinctive landscapes and colours; Indigenous art is a prized export commodity; writers and film-makers capture the guises of a multi-cultural Australia; popular entertainers sing with an Australian accent; and musicians freely fuse styles and traditions. But when this shy, naïve youth from provincial Tasmania set out on his musical journey in the 1950s, even a career as a composer was unthinkable, except as an adjunct to a day-job performing, broadcasting or teaching. The alternative was to go overseas, a pathway that Sculthorpe briefly followed as a scholarship student to Oxford from 1958 to 1960 but rejected as temperamentally unsuitable.

As a child, Peter Sculthorpe set about writing an Aboriginal dictionary and 'painted' his own environment in musical jottings, poems and drawings, all still lovingly kept in his archive at the National Library of Australia and already suggestive of his inner fascination with place. Sculthorpe's individual voice speaks early on, in the *Sonatina for Piano* (1954), the *Irkanda* series (1955–61), the Sixth String Quartet (1964–65) and the *Sun Music* series (1965–69), which attracted early international prominence. But it was from the mid-1970s that his music increasingly found its Australian context, either through direct reference to location or through imagined 'dreaming' of place, in works such as *Port Essington, Earth Cry, Mangrove, Kakadu, Nourlangie, Great Sandy Island*.

Sculthorpe's musical voice is mostly characterised as sparse, reflective, brooding and eerie. The language seems pared back to the bare essence, static and inhabiting a 'flat' sound-world, derived, he claims, from the monotonous delivery of Australian speech. Characteristically the music moves in slow, spacious blocks of sound, often coloured by distinctive instrumental formations and overlaid with a distinguishable melody of limited range: a kind of impassioned utterance that the listener comes to recognise through repetition. Ideas are abruptly juxtaposed from one section to another, rather than subjected to development or variation. Sculthorpe constructs through sound his perception of a remote and uncompromising ancient land of extreme contrasts, one in which space, isolation and loneliness prevail.

The Australian idiom recurs as mottos: the impassioned screeches of seagulls, the shimmering sound-clusters associated with the sun, the contours of melody that trace a particular horizon. With its flat intervals the *Djilile* melody, borrowed from Arnhem Land, threads through Sculthorpe's works from 1974, much like a 'songline'. More recently, the addition of semi-improvised rhythmic drones and chants of the didjeridu have given life to new versions of earlier works, many in collaboration with the Indigenous player William Barton.

Works like the string quartets are ripe for such reinvention. They are already deeply immersed in Sculthorpe's personal sound-world: ritualistic chants, drones, laments, dances, textures drawn upon as sources of inspiration from non-European cultural traditions. He sees no disparity in drawing equally from Japanese gagaku, Balinese gamelan or Native American chants, from transplanted colonial roots or Aboriginal Australia, and his endless fascination with visual or aural sources for musical inspiration knows no borders.

Such diverse stimuli, though, are always absorbed into the distinctive Sculthorpe voice and, in turn, take on their own cultural meaning. In his choral *Requiem*, commissioned for the 2004 Adelaide Festival of Arts, Sculthorpe invokes, layers and inverts the timeless rituals of two cultures. The Latin text and chants of the Catholic 'Mass for the Dead' are counterpointed with ancient Aboriginal rites articulated in the virtuosic chanting of the didjeridu. For the first time, Sculthorpe explicitly composes for this solo instrument and frees himself from the musical constraints which he, like fellow composers, often felt when addressing Indigenous culture. In the *Requiem*, the Indigenous voice is given equality and independence through the didjeridu, while framed within the heritage of European settlement. This is poignantly referenced through the use of the *Maranoa Lullaby*, the only Aboriginal song to be regularly taught to school-children from the 1930s and first arranged by Sculthorpe during his student years at the University of Melbourne.

The *Requiem* signifies Sculthorpe's deeply personal, yet eloquently public journey towards a musical reconciliation of contested cultural inheritance, a reconciliation of his own spiritual and musical connections with a multiplicity of traditions and contexts. These belie any purely intellectual or singular pursuit of what 'Australian-ness' in music should or might be. In time, Peter Sculthorpe's ultimate gift to Australian culture may be the freedom he has forged for younger generations, many of whom he has taught and nurtured, to explore their own musical voices and be celebrated as Australian composers in their own land while asserting a place on the global stage. ■

the dreaming . . . or not?

ROLF de HEER

I dislike the expression 'the Dreaming', much as I dislike the expression 'the Dreamtime'. In my opinion they should both be eradicated from any usage remotely connected with the belief systems of Australian Indigenous people.

I came to Australia in 1959 as an eight-year-old, not knowing a word of English. I learnt my new language quickly, almost revelled in it. I read voraciously, forgot my Dutch, and within a couple of years English was my best subject. I regularly topped the class against those who had spoken it all their lives.

It was late in primary school that the terms 'the Dreaming' and 'the Dreamtime' first came to my notice. The entire and ostensibly true history of Aboriginals in Australia was given to us in the form of a comic, complete with speech balloons and happy Aboriginals (although they did occasionally spear a white person and were severely punished for such transgressions).

I had no cause to question any of this. Kenny Hamilton, in another class, was of Aboriginal descent, and he seemed pretty happy, so obviously this is how things were. And my first conceptual imaginings of what 'Dreaming' and 'Dreamtime' might really mean fitted pretty well with what I read in the comic: a simple and childlike people, happily sitting in humpies dreaming of the past.

It's difficult to escape this imagery, created by words whose meaning we first learn in an entirely different context. It's not imagery Australian Indigenous people asked for, or propagated until they were told that these were the words to use in English. And one would have to say that the imagery is damaging to Western perceptions and preconceptions of Aboriginal people and culture, and actually a fair distance removed from the reality.

The word 'Dreamtime' first came to prominence in 1896, used by the famed 'anthropologists' Spencer and Gillen. Gillen supposedly coined the word, and Spencer, the senior member of the duo, popularised it. Interestingly, neither was actually an anthropologist by trade, and certainly neither of them was a linguist.

Spencer was an evolutionary botanist, who had signed onto the Horn Scientific Expedition to Central Australia as a zoologist and photographer. Gillen was even further from the profession of anthropological linguistics; he was, and always had been, a postmaster, which presumably qualified him for his secondary job as protector of Aboriginals.

'Dreamtime' is said by Spencer and Gillen to be a rough translation of the Aranda word 'alcheringa', but linguists since have argued that this was arrived at through a grammatical error made by them. Strehlow, a contemporary of Spencer and Gillen and a recognised authority on the Aranda language at the time, argued that the Aranda had no word for 'dream' as an abstract.

Despite attempts at different translations of 'alcheringa' (there's argument about it being an Aranda word at all), and similar or equivalent words from other Aboriginal languages ('the distant past when the world was created', 'the world dawn', 'dawn of the world') 'Dreamtime', and 'the Dreaming' along with it, has stuck, in both anthropological and common usage.

The problem I've found with concepts such as these, and many others, is that there's simply no way to translate them from an Aboriginal language into English, because the words and ideas are about a different universe than the one we inhabit. The same is true for the reverse.

We think we get good clues as to what this great universe might be like, philosophical clues such as the connectedness of all things, clues from the rich ceremonial life, the deep engagement with the spirit world. But these are false clues, because they ignore the essence of the problem . . . We have no access to the structure and meaning of the thinking that such a different way of seeing the universe brings about, because we can only analyse it with our structure of thinking, our ways of ascribing meaning.

Problematical, too, is the use of the word 'Dreaming' across all the different Indigenous belief systems – different because there simply isn't just one homogenous belief system, but substantial variations from people to people. The word, its more common meaning referring to a very particular process of mind, gives a false sense of universality, of sameness, of all Australian Indigenous people, whereas in truth there are huge cultural differences between, say, a Western Desert tribe and the Yolngu of Arnhem Land. This false universality, in turn, supports the disastrous 'one solution fits all' mentality of any government struggling to come to terms with Indigenous issues.

During my time with Aboriginal people, particularly those of Arnhem Land, I've gradually replaced 'Dreamtime' with the simple (and of intended lesser meaning) 'Creation Time', since most of the stories associated with the belief system relate exactly to that. Creation Time was a time of anything but dreaming – it was a time of intense physical and conceptual activity.

As God is real to many people, and the Big Bang beginnings of the Universe real to many others, so is Creation Time real to many Indigenous Australians. And as much as white Anglicans or Catholics don't sit dreaming about events in Genesis, neither do Indigenous people sit dreaming of Creation Time. ■

robert menzies' 'the forgotten people' broadcast

JUDITH BRETT

Robert Menzies was a consummate political communicator. Like Franklin Roosevelt with his 'fireside chats' to Depression America, he used radio to talk intimately to voters about their private hopes and fears, his well-modulated voice coming through the wireless into their kitchens and lounge rooms. On Friday 22 May 1942, he made an evening radio broadcast to 'the forgotten people', one of a weekly series during 1942 and 1943 in which he reflected on the relevance of the values of his side of politics to wartime Australia and the post-war future. Menzies had resigned as Prime Minister the previous August and the government fell soon after to Labor. He was at his lowest ebb, politically. That inspired him. While the new Labor government was thriving on wartime mobilisation, Menzies was searching for touchstones that would ring true with the electorate, for words that would remake him and his side of politics.

The term 'the forgotten people' was a transformation of 'the forgotten class', a description of the middle class since the nineteenth century, which captured its propensity to grievance as it struggled for political space between the rich and powerful and the increasingly well organised working class. By replacing the term 'class' with 'people', Menzies broadened its potential appeal. What was crucial for the way Menzies defined the middle class was not who was included but *why*.

The speech is a paean of praises for middle-class virtues, enumerated through the organising trope of its 'responsibility for homes – homes material, homes human and homes spiritual'. Attached to 'homes material' are the virtues of frugality and patriotism; to 'homes human', ambition for one's children; and to 'homes spiritual', commitment to independence and respect for liberal education and cultural achievement. Crucial to the logic of the speech is that members of the middle class possess these virtues as individuals. Being middle class is not based on a person's economic role, as in Labor's class-based schema. Rather, it is based on strength of character, respectability and sense of responsibility – anyone can possess these qualities, no matter what their job or level of material wealth. It is who one is, not what one does, that defines one's social worth. The real life of the nation is to be found 'in the homes of people who are nameless and unadvertised and who, whatever their individual conviction or dogma, see in their children their greatest contribution to the immortality of the human race.'

Talking to people in their homes about the importance of their home-life, Menzies was inviting listeners to identify their political interests not with their class-based economic role and the conflicts of the workplace, which was Labor's turf, but with their domestic selves – their private pleasures and ambitions. The broadcast spoke especially to women's home- and family-centred lives, and their responsibility for the moral education of children. For most of the twentieth century the Liberal Party enjoyed an electoral advantage among women, and Mr Menzies was a particular favourite.

Out of power when he wrote it, Menzies is reflective and personal in this speech as he delves into his own experience for imagery to describe middle-class virtue. His parents were the prototypes of the frugal, community-minded people who 'see in their children their greatest contribution to the immortality of their race'. The speech can be seen as a turning point in his political career, the moment when he accepted that his political future lay here in Australia, not at the centre of the British Empire in London. After his humiliating resignation less than a year earlier, Menzies could well have chosen to leave politics. In this speech we see him recommitting himself to a political constituency. A year later he began work on the formation of a new non-Labor party: the Liberal Party of Australia. Menzies' capacity to creatively rework non-Labor's political philosophy for the changed post-war world is one of the main reasons he became the first leader of the new party.

The speech was circulated as a pamphlet and became the title essay in a collection of Menzies' radio broadcasts published in 1943. Its longevity, however, owes less to its impact at the time than to the way it foreshadowed the place of home and family in post-war Australia, and Menzies' domination of the nation's politics from 1949 until his retirement in 1967. As the Australian economy settled into the long boom, increased affluence and better education dissolved the pre-war class boundaries and antagonisms. People moved into the spreading new suburbs to buy or build their homes and raise their children, and the term middle class lost its exclusivity to become a synonym for 'normal' or 'average'. The speech is remembered for its praise of home and family as universal values, and this is crucial to its political logic; but it also carries a nasty class disdain as it attacks the commitment to equality in the expanding welfare state.

In 1949 Menzies and the new Liberal Party defeated Labor in what turned out to be a watershed election. Labor did not return to government until 1972. This was the Liberal Party's golden age, and Menzies was its hero. Retrospectively, 'The Forgotten People' became a foundational moment. ∎

the sydney harbour bridge

PETER SPEARRITT

Anyone who has ever experienced a flood or queued for hours to get a berth on a vehicular ferry knows the utility of a good bridge. Since the 1840s Sydneysiders had been queuing at Dawes Point and Milsons Point to move themselves, if not their horses and carts, from one side of the harbour to the other.

By the time the Sydney Harbour Bridge got parliamentary approval in 1922, bridge builders in the United Kingdom, Canada and the United States had produced wondrous steel structures, high enough to let shipping clear and strong enough to support both trains and the rising tide of motor traffic.

When the NSW government embarked on the Harbour Bridge, choosing an arch rather than a cantilever design, Australia had little industrial capacity beyond mining, brewing and food manufacture. The BHP steelworks at Newcastle was just seven years old, so most of the steel had to be imported from the UK. And the bridge would be paid for by a toll and contributions from the nearby local councils.

Sydney's grandest nineteenth-century building, its Garden Palace, didn't manage to survive a fire just three years after its completion. Melbourne's grandest structure, the Royal Exhibition Building, seemed-old fashioned as soon as it began exhibiting. Sydney and Melbourne both had palatial railway stations, a handful of big hotels and emporiums, a few grand churches, but no skyscrapers.

So imagine the excitement when the bridge arches could be seen growing from both sides of the harbour. Many boys – and even some girls – were given Meccano sets to make their own versions of the Harbour Bridge. Sydneysiders could see the bridge from many vantage points, from North Head to Bankstown. During its seven years of construction, from 1925 to 1932, the fifty million people a year who travelled on ferries marvelled at the bravery of the workmen, who had no safety apparatus, and the majesty of the steel structure. In 1930 illegal bets were placed on whether the two arches would meet or not. They did, and then the roadway, incorporating tram tracks and rail tracks, was hung from the main arch.

British publishers were quick to claim the bridge as a triumph of British engineering, while Australian reactions were summed up in the phrase, 'still building Australia'. In 1929 controversy erupted about whether Dr J.J.C. Bradfield, the Queensland-born engineer in charge of the bridge project and electrification of the suburban railway system, or Ralph Freeman, the engineer for the British contractors Dorman Long and Co, could best be described as the designer of the bridge. At least the stone in the pylons came unambiguously from the NSW south-coast town of Moruya, even if Scottish stonemasons had to be imported to cut and dress the granite.

American newspapers and magazines ignored the bridge, which didn't even make it to the standard US list of the Seven Wonders of the Modern World. The society that produced the Empire State Building also managed to build the Bayonne Bridge between Staten Island and New Jersey, deliberately making it twenty-five inches longer than the Harbour Bridge. Sydney was left claiming the widest and the heaviest arch bridge, not the longest. But these statistics soon paled into insignificance, compared to the upset opening on 19 March 1932, when Ken Hall sent the world's newspapers his cameraman's still of Captain de

Groot cutting the ribbon before Premier Jack Lang could get to it. Many of the one million people who walked across the Bridge that day didn't find out about de Groot's mounted coup until they read the evening newspapers.

By the 1950s the bridge, with its cars, trains, trams, trucks and pedestrians, was viewed as so utilitarian that the Department of Main Roads didn't even bother to steam-clean the grime-covered pylons. That very same department attempted to add a ninth lane to the bridge in 1982, the year of its fiftieth anniversary, but by then it had become Australia's first unquestionably iconic structure, featuring in the work of novelists, photographers, filmmakers and artists, from Christina Stead and Ken Hall to Harold Cazneaux, Max Dupain, Martin Sharp and Brett Whiteley. Half a million people walked across it to mark its fiftieth anniversary. The roadway has been open to the people for a reconciliation march and subsequent anniversaries. Since 1998 over one and a half million people have walked over the arch itself, at considerable expense, in the world's first and most successful bridge climbing operation. Pedestrians can still walk over the eastern pathway without charge, as can cyclists riding on the western pathway.

Tolls have been charged on the bridge ever since it opened, giving us a unique insight into changing transport patterns. Until the late 1950s, many more people crossed the bridge by train, tram or bus than by private motor vehicle. Car and truck crossings peaked in 1990 and have since fallen with the opening of the Harbour Tunnel in 1992. Railway patronage has increased in recent years and rail now carries as many people across the bridge as drive through the Harbour Tunnel.

The Harbour Bridge has long been Australia's most recognised symbol, much to the chagrin of Melburnians. With the addition of the Opera House, the two structures continue to dominate Australia's overseas promotion, from the Sydney Olympic Games in 2000 to the New Year's Eve fireworks, the only Australian pyrotechnics to feature on the world television stage. The bridge has both practical utility and symbolic power. 'The arch that cut the skies' still dominates Sydney's landscape and imagination, for visitors and locals alike. ∎

the game

MARTIN FLANAGAN

Picasso said you have to go to a lot of bullfights to see a great bullfight. So, too, with Australian football. What do I mean by a 'great' game? One which is transcendent in that it makes me forget everything but the action unfolding before my eyes. I had a sense of it, for example, in the 2005 grand final between Sydney and West Coast. All these great contests going on all over the ground which, for the reason outlined above, is as far as I can see. That day had a mythical conclusion, too. To understand it you need to know that it's difficult to run in perpendicular to the line of flight of a ball and mark it. You need to further understand another five or so players are trying to catch it. Immortality awaits any who succeeds in doing so. Enter Leo Barry perpendicular to the line of flight. Leo is a defender with dash. He should knock the ball to ground. He doesn't. He marks, snatching it from the hands of an oncoming rush of players. The siren sounds. The Swans have won for the first time in 72 years. Get your mind around that. My old man says, 'I barracked for them when they won their first premiership. I was 19. I barracked for them when they won their second premiership. I was 91'.

That's another reason footy's great for me. It's my father's game and his father's before him. My grandfather could write no more than his name and was the grandson of a convict. Between the convict and my grandfather, my family history got cut off, as happened in Tasmanian convict families. For me, it meant a massive loss of culture, of stories from that other time and place, maybe even of language. A couple of years ago when I went back to Elphin, the town the Flanagans come from in Ireland, I met Pat Flanagan (the name also of my grandfather and my eldest brother). This Irish Pat Flanagan said to me, 'The Flanagans are interested in four things – football, politics, horses and cattle.' When I gave a copy of one of my books, *The Game in Time of War,* to the best player in the Elphin Gaelic football team he looked at its cover and said to me, 'But how do I know you are this Martin Flanagan?' And he had a point. I met Martin Flanagan my first night in Elphin. He's a builder.

And what's also great about footy is that it takes you places you never expect to go. Places of the mind. I have a favourite bush setting in Victoria that I hardly talk about – a natural bush setting with ancient eucalypts. Too hard to explain. I'm in a car with Michael Long. A whitefeller and a blackfeller are crossing the continent, driving from Melbourne to Darwin, and just as we pass my secret place he says to me, 'What's your favourite place in Victoria, Martin?', like he's sensed it. The game has taken me other places too, like South Africa. The game beats with a pure heart over there. They met Michael Long with a special song, like he was a great warrior being welcomed to their land. The South African coach, Mtutu Hlomela, had come to Australia on a soccer scholarship and was mistakenly sent to Sturt Football Club in Adelaide where they played the game with an odd-shaped ball. Mtutu stayed. The first big game he saw – the 1993 preliminary final between Essendon and Adelaide (by my standards, a great game) – was won by a black man, Michael Long. The next week the same man danced all over the opposition, a blackfeller dance as the nation watched and applauded, seeing Aboriginal art and mastery in that modern stadium. Australian football has understood the creative potential of a relationship with black Australia since 1993, maybe a lot longer. That's another thing that's great about the game. Hearing a half-time address in Pitjantjatjara and not understanding a word and understanding every word because you understand the rhythm of the speech, the ancient chant which stirs young men to action.

If I keep going I'll start another chapter, this one about Latrobe Football Club in Tasmania. Both my grandfathers may have played for Latrobe. So did

Ivor Warne-Smith, later to win two Brownlow medals with Melbourne. I could tell you lots of stories from that point, but perhaps in this context one will do. In the early 1920s, the North-west went to play Hobart in Hobart. You've got to understand how hated the south was in the north of the state, but in football they nearly always won. But this day Warne Smith was playing. The Latrobe champion was injured early, limped on, but the South yet again won the day. That was the only time in his wholly Tasmanian life my grandfather saw Hobart, the biggest city in his world. My grandmother never did. That's the other thing about footy. It's great what you get to hear, listening to footy stories. ■

hurley on ice

STEPHEN MARTIN

It's one of the greatest images of the twentieth century, taken by one of the century's best Antarctic photographers, James Francis Hurley. In the dark of a winter night, the *Endurance,* rigging and decks frosted with rime, sits fast in the ice of the Weddell Sea, Antarctica. The ship is upright and, more in hope than expectation, it's still tethered to the frozen sea. The contrast between the night sky and the magnesium-flare-lit ship is stark, beautiful and menacing. It's a photograph that illustrates one of the best adventure stories of all time; one that is redolent with shipwreck, privation, courage and survival against the natural odds of Antarctica.

Hurley's diary for the night, 27 August 1915, reads:

During the night take flashlight of ship beset by pressure. This necessitated some 20 flashes, one behind each salient hummock, no less than 10 of the flashes being required to satisfactorily illuminate the ship herself. Half blinded after the successive flashes, I lost my bearing amidst the hummocks, bumping shins against projecting ice points & stumbling into deep snow drifts.

This is the Antarctic Hurley we all know: adventurous, persistent, technically superb and absolutely dedicated to his pursuit of the perfect shot. Hurley the great photographer.

In 1919, after the adventures of the *Endurance* expedition and looking back through the prism of war experience, Hurley wrote about polar exploration:

> It appeals to me because it is a life of thrilling excitement where only too frequently one's grip of life on this planet depends on the judgment and resource of the individual, and, secondly and principally, because Antarctica is a world of transcendent beauty, infinite pictorial scope, and a virgin field, which call forth one's best effort. There are joys, too, of the combat, for every negative has to be won from a relentless and unsympathetic nature, and produced under unprecedented circumstances.

Hurley's fascination with Antarctica probably began when he visited the *Nimrod*, Shackleton's expedition vessel, in 1909. He was official photographer of the remarkable Trans Antarctic Expedition (1914–1917) when he took the flashlight night photo of the *Endurance* under pressure. The quality and drama of his images are now inseparable from the epic scope of that adventure – the widespread familiarity of the tale is due in no small part to Hurley's work.

Two years earlier he was with Douglas Mawson's Australasian Antarctic Expedition (AAE) 1911–1914 as documentary photographer. After one year with this expedition, he returned to the settled world with beautiful and dramatic images of a far-off exotic place. His cinematic footage of the expedition, cobbled together and later known as *Home of the Blizzard*, featured images of men building a life in the white wilds of the far south. Screening to fascinated audiences even before the main party returned, Hurley was offering a modern, visual meaning to Antarctica while fashioning himself as an entrepreneur extraordinaire.

Hurley's photographs of the Mawson expedition were widely distributed and exhibited. The exhibition at the London Fine Art Society in 1915 helped him to move from his growing reputation as a competent and dramatic photographer of landscapes to a world figure.

It was this fame, particularly the reaction to *Home of the Blizzard,* that attracted Sir Ernest Shackleton, keen to have images and movies of his own adventures to sell and defray expedition costs – and let it be said, to ensure the fame of Shackleton's own Antarctic exploits. Joining the *Endurance* in 1914, Hurley became an integral part of the story and its telling. His footage of the expedition, including the slow and tortuous crushing of the ship, was released as *In the Grip of the Polar Ice* in 1915. The film has captured audiences ever since.

Traits of greatness include energy and persistence. Hurley pursued his work with a vitality that reminded South African journalist Laurens van der Post of a modern 'Elizabethan'. He was a mix of adventurer, artist, writer and entrepreneur. His work was made not simply for art's sake, or for celebrity, although this helped – he worked for money to keep going, to keep Hurley Inc on the road. He possessed the capacity for intense concentration. He loved his work. On his first experience of the subantarctic, on Macquarie Island in 1911, he was totally absorbed in the task. Fellow expeditioner Archibald McLean described him as working in a kind of 'photographic ecstasy'. He was caught in a comparable intensity, though it might better be called 'agony', when he took his war photos on the Western Front in 1917–1918. On the Western Front he was called the 'mad photographer'.

Antarcticans and visitors draw inspiration from Hurley's images of the south. Those familiar with the continent and its human stories find a comforting reference. Those who aren't see some part of the continent's mystery explained: they receive a sense of knowledge and experience, but it's a perception that retains an awe and otherworldliness of a land of ice. Hurley's Antarctic photography included shots of the expeditioners surviving against great odds, but also the more mundane, people at work or pursuing everyday lives, as much as one can in Antarctica. His characters now seem universal – heroes yet vulnerable and all-too-human, like beings from Greek mythology.

At his best Hurley was one of the finest photographers of Antarctica, imaging a land and its wildlife with precision and drama. But he was also a shaper of stories, giving form and light and perspective to epic, enduring tales of exploration. His photography of people in the ice, such as the *Endurance* image, confirm his talent and mark his greatness. ∎

the freedom ride

ANN CURTHOYS

The Freedom Ride helped change the course of Australian history. Not on its
own, of course, and not easily, but it did make a difference. It is one of the delights
of my life that I was there, saw what happened, helped in a small way to make it
happen, and later had the opportunity to write a book about the events, called
Freedom Ride: A Freedom Rider Remembers.

The original Freedom Ride took place in February 1965, and there were
some follow-up trips so that sometimes people speak of the 'Freedom Rides'. The
first Freedom Ride, however, is the one that was truly an 'Australian Great'. It was
a two-week bus trip by students from the University of Sydney, which travelled
around country towns in New South Wales protesting against discrimination
against Indigenous people. The students confronted the long-standing and
ongoing exclusion in certain country towns of Aboriginal people from the
facilities that everyone else enjoyed – especially cinemas, swimming pools, RSL
clubs. They also protested about poor housing conditions, and the exclusion
of Aboriginal people from houses in town. Despite a government policy of
assimilation that emphasised, in theory at least, that Aboriginal people should be
included in the everyday life of the society as full citizens – in schools, workplaces,
leisure places and as voting citizens – there were throughout Australian society
deeply entrenched habits of racism, segregation and exclusion. Most whites in
country towns thought of the towns as theirs and the Aboriginal people who

lived on the edges as intruders, people who had to be kept out or at least severely circumscribed and controlled.

In the mid 1960s many Aboriginal people were demanding a change. They wanted genuinely equal treatment, with full access to houses in town, jobs, education, and public spaces. They also wanted to retain their identity as Aboriginal people, and especially their family relationships and connection to their own country. They wanted an end to racism and in its place recognition and respect. Signs of this changing mood among Aboriginal people, and also among some white people who sought a more egalitarian society, included the development of a range of mixed-race organisations fighting for Aboriginal rights. During the 1960s the growing Aboriginal rights movement waged campaigns for employment opportunities, equal wages, improvements in housing, and much else.

One of the leaders in this growing movement was Charles Perkins, an Arrernte man and former soccer player who moved from Adelaide to Sydney in 1962 and subsequently decided he wanted a university education. His enrolment at the University of Sydney in 1963 helped bring together two emerging forces that were to change Australian society: the Aboriginal rights movement and student radicalism. Also starting at the university that year was Gary Williams, a Gumbaynggir man who had just completed his Leaving Certificate. The presence of these two Aboriginal students was a catalyst for change. During 1964 signs of the increasing levels of student radicalism on questions of racial equality included a massive demonstration in support of African American Civil Rights and a concert in Hyde Park during National Aborigines Week. From these and other activities emerged the idea of having a Freedom Ride on the model of the Freedom Rides in the US in 1961, which had protested against segregated transportation facilities, attracting huge opposition but succeeding in their immediate aims. The Australian Freedom Ride, however, was to have a broader focus: the students would travel to country towns already known for their discriminatory behaviour and protest against any forms of discrimination they could find.

The Freedom Ride bus left Sydney on 12 February 1965. On board were 29 students, including Charles Perkins and Gary Williams. Some left during the two week trip to towns like Wellington, Gulargambone, Dubbo, Walgett, Moree, Boggabilla, Grafton, Lismore, Bowraville, Kempsey and Taree, and others joined later. Over the two weeks there were thirty-three freedom riders, eleven of them women. The average age was just 19. The freedom ride went through Orange, Wellington and Dubbo without incident, but when it arrived at Walgett it was a different story.

The students protested against the practice of the local RSL club of excluding Aboriginal ex-servicemen from the club, sometimes even on Anzac Day. Charlie Perkins understood the symbolic significance of this exclusion, for it was important to Aboriginal people in the area to have their war service remembered and valued. To reject ex-servicemen was truly to reject Aboriginal people altogether. The line of students holding up placards outside the local RSL club attracted huge crowds, leading to much public argument and speech making. When the students left town, the son of a local grazier attempted to run them off the road. The roads had deep ditches alongside, and to run off the road could well have meant turning the bus over. Unfortunately for the local white townsfolk, there was a *Sydney Morning Herald* cadet journalist in town, and the incident got full coverage in the urban newspapers. What made the news was not so much the student protest as the white hostility towards them, suggesting that racial segregation and exclusion were indeed the status quo and the local whites would fight hard to keep it that way.

Journalists from a number of newspapers rushed to join the bus, ensuring massive media coverage of the Freedom Ride from then on. At the next town, Moree, the focus of interest was the swimming pool, from which Aboriginal people were excluded (except for school children during school hours). The students took Aboriginal children to the pool and held a large public meeting in the town on the issue of racial discrimination. Believing the council management, who owned pool, had agreed to desegregate it, they moved on to Boggabilla. When they later learnt that Aboriginal children were again being excluded, they returned to Moree. On this second visit, the students again took some Aboriginal children to the pool and demanded they be allowed in. This time, they were refused. The students kept asking, the pool officials kept refusing, and a huge crowd surrounded them. There was immense hostility towards the students, much verbal abuse, and a little physical violence. In an increasingly tense atmosphere, representatives of both the council and the students met and negotiated a settlement. The regulation keeping Aboriginals out of the pool would be rescinded and the students would leave town.

The Freedom Ride continued holding demonstrations in other towns. But in one sense, its job was already done. The media throughout the country – print, radio, and television – was discussing the issues, and there was quite some soul-searching about the poor conditions under which Aboriginal people lived, the reasons for it and the solutions. The Moree and Kempsey pools were desegregated, and eventually so too was the Walgett RSL Club. Charles Perkins became a well-known Aboriginal leader, and student support for Aboriginal activism continued for many years; indeed it continues still. The Freedom Ride was followed by the eventually successful campaign to change the Australian Constitution to allow Commonwealth involvement in Aboriginal policy, as confirmed by the Referendum of 1967. Many other campaigns followed, and the concerns of the Freedom Ride were overtaken by other demands, especially land rights and other forms of organisation.

The Freedom Ride remains important as that moment highlighted publicly the depth of continuing racism and social disadvantage. The shock the Freedom Ride gave to the political system continues to be felt to this day. ∎

christina stead

HAZEL ROWLEY

Her father, a naturalist, would entertain her with stories about the outback, the first Australians and their corroborees, Captain Cook's travels, convict ships and the giant kangaroos that used to roam the mud swamps. The menagerie behind their house in Watsons Bay, Sydney, contained an echidna, emu, venomous black snakes and a diamond snake, whose erratic eating habits David Stead noted carefully. Stead was a playful man, who loved children but would cruelly taunt and manipulate them, and he left his eldest daughter with deep scars. Nevertheless, Christina Stead would always feel grateful to her father for teaching her to swim in the 'ocean of story'.

Christina Stead was thirty-six when she sat down in her dark Manhattan apartment to write *The Man Who Loved Children,* based on her own childhood. For months she slept badly and wept uncontrollably. It was a 'snake's life', she told a friend, to shed her skin as she was doing. Her choice of image – more evocative of her Sydney childhood than her life in New York – suggests she had not entirely managed to do so. Her father, from the other side of the world, still cast a large shadow on her life.

Stead would always call herself a 'naturalist writer'. As she saw it, her task as a writer was to observe people, objectively, without moral judgement. ('When you're a little girl and you look in an aquarium and you see fish doing this and that ... you don't criticise and say they should do something else. And that's the way in which I was brought up.') Her curiosity about people was unquenchable, and her greatest strength as a writer was definitely character portrayal, with a remarkable flair for rendering voice. With her closest friends, she would invariably feel the same deep ambivalence – powerful admiration combined with resentment – that she felt towards her father. When these friends became models for characters in her fiction, she would work herself into a lather of emotion and write at white heat. Most of Christina Stead's novels seethe with rage, and yet they are devoid of moral colouring. It leaves her readers feeling disoriented, a little dizzy.

Christina Stead's autobiographical novel *For Love Alone* makes it clear what it cost her to leave Australia at the age of twenty-six, all alone, on that six-week trip across the world, headed for the unknown. She was a virgin, and had scarcely experienced love, though she took with her a pile of letters from a young man who had left for London two years earlier. It was March 28, 1928, when she stood on deck waving goodbye to her family, and she would never see her father again. She would not return to Australia until 1969, when she was sixty-seven and an internationally famous writer.

Christina Stead's young man jilted her soon after she arrived in London (just as Teresa's young man does in the novel), but Stead had meanwhile landed a secretarial job with a grain company, and her boss – a New Yorker of German Jewish origin – would become her companion (he was already married) and eventually her husband. With Bill Blech, her 'Wandering Jew', Stead moved between London, Paris, Antwerp and New York, and for seven years they shifted restlessly around France, Switzerland and Italy. Stead's fiction is set all over the place, and her characters are often wanderers.

When I was writing Stead's biography in the 1980s, I met several of the people on whom Stead had based her characters, and it was a bewildering experience. She had captured their voices so exactly, it was as if they had walked out of the novel at me. Even today, I will be in Watsons Bay looking out at the Pacific or I'll see fireflies in the American countryside, and a flutter of excitement comes over me and I'll think of *For Love Alone* or *The People with the Dogs* or another of Stead's novels. The inspiration I feel comes both from the writing itself, its sheer dazzling brilliance, and the writer – her courage, her cultural adaptability, her powers of observation and her wide-open horizons.

I would argue that no writer anywhere in the world has been more cosmopolitan than Christina Stead, with such a genius for portraying different cultures and voices. She was a great Australian writer, who had a talent for feeling at home anywhere. Her natural habitat was, quite simply, the ocean of story. ■

expats – thoughts from a broad

KATHY LETTE

When I first moved to England twenty years ago, Australians were still seen as bad seeds; the Irish of the Pacific; a recessive gene. We were the *Illiterati* – people who could only use the word 'opera' next to the word 'soap'. It was presumed an Australian's only record collections were *criminal* – not classical. It was also assumed that our main topic of conversation revolved around how long we had to go on parole, with the occasional digression into our dating history – beginning with pets and other animals.

Actually, it took me a while to ascertain the true level of antipathy towards Antipodeans because nobody speaks English in England. They speak Euphemism. If you're going to survive in the Mother Country as an expat, the first lesson you should learn is that visitors need those little United Nations translation headphones to decode conversations. 'Oh you Australians, you're so *refreshing*', for example, may lull you into the belief that your hosts really, really like you. Wrong. What that comment *actually* means is 'rack off you loud-mouthed Colonial nymphomaniac'.

You see, the English cultural commissars have a condescension chromosome. Many have been at Oxford for so long they've got ivy growing up the backs of their legs. And what they've graduated in is Advanced Smugness. Since moving to London, all I do is look up noses – even noses of people shorter than me! Oh yes, there's nothing like being spoken down to by complete acquaintances – especially when having your grammar corrected.

Of course, the reason the place is crawling with Conan the Grammarians is all to do with breeding. In Australia breeding is something we do with sheep. Aussie boys take note: English women aren't looking for *Mr* Right, but Lord, Baron, *Marquis* Right at the very least. (Personally, I prefer the Aussie approach of looking for Mr Wrong or Mr Kinda-okay or Mr Everyone-else-has-gone-home-so-you'll-have-to-do.) But the British actually publish a book called *Debrett's,* which details people's property and pedigree. In truth, the upper class prefers their pedigree dogs to people. I mean, they keep their canines at home and send their kids off to high-class kennels called Eton and Harrow where they're taught to use expressions such as 'she's not one of us' and 'he's getting above himself'.

Of course, it's the Royal Family who are above us all. The Windsors put the fun into dysfunctional. In fact, they make the Osbournes look well-adjusted. With voices brittle enough to qualify for osteoporosis pills and facial expressions by taxidermy, they are the lynchpin of the class system. Despite my allergy to these winners in the Lucky Sperm Competition (I mean, how would you feel about hereditary doctors, dentists and authors?) I must admit a soft spot for Prince Charles. Actually, I've liked him ever since he wanted to be a tampon . . . Although it does seem to be a metaphor for his entire life – *always in the right place at the wrong time.* If you mention the Queen to most Aussie kids, they think you're talking about Elton John. Which makes me hopeful that one day Australia will vote to become a Republic and come in from the Reign. And then England will become our brother, rather than our mother nation, and perhaps their cultural condescension will ease? (Yeah, right, and Elton has his own hair.)

Okay, you expat-in-training, that's enough food for thought. What about the actual tucker? All I can say about English gastronomy is that this is the nation who took jelly and eels and said, 'Hey! Let's put them together!' With a few expensive exceptions, eat in most English restaurants and pretty soon your head will no longer be on speaking terms with your stomach.

Worse than the sado-mastication is the fact that the English are all members of a Mutual Aberration Society. In Australia, the only thing we girls like to whip is cream. But be warned: years of boarding school means that the Englishman of your dreams may pretend to wear pinstriped underpants but probably runs off to brothels at night to be whipped with bits of wet lettuce. (Well, the winters are long and Monopoly and Scrabble do get so dull after a while . . .)

There are many other imperative expat survival tips. Did you know that the English think optimism is an eye disease? That they don't do anything spontaneous without a warning? But there are also some good points to living here. In Australia, we lie down in front of bulldozers to protect heritage-listed buildings constructed in, say, 1967. London has a host of ghosts, every nook and cranny haemorrhaging history. And then there's the galleries, the theatre, the museums . . . In England you learn to conquer the Great Indoors.

But what an Aussie expat will *never* get used to is the winter. For six months of the year, it's dark by 3.30 pm and all of London takes on the wan, grey, sepia light of a pre-war photograph: bare trees straggling up hills like hairs in an unshaven armpit. Living under that oppressive grey duvet of rain clouds, you miss being drenched in a wash of syrupy sunlight, as you lie supine on the golden Sydney sands. You ache for those huge azure skies with curlicues of creamy clouds. You long for the wattle-scented winds, warm as an embrace . . . (Homesick? Moi? You bloody betcha! As my family won't leave London, my plan is to kill a corgi and get deported.)

But my best expat survival tip of all is this: if an English person makes some derisory comment about Australia's inauspicious beginnings, pass on what my grandma said when I told her I was moving to London. 'England? Oh you can't go there, dear. That's where all those terrible convicts came from!' ∎

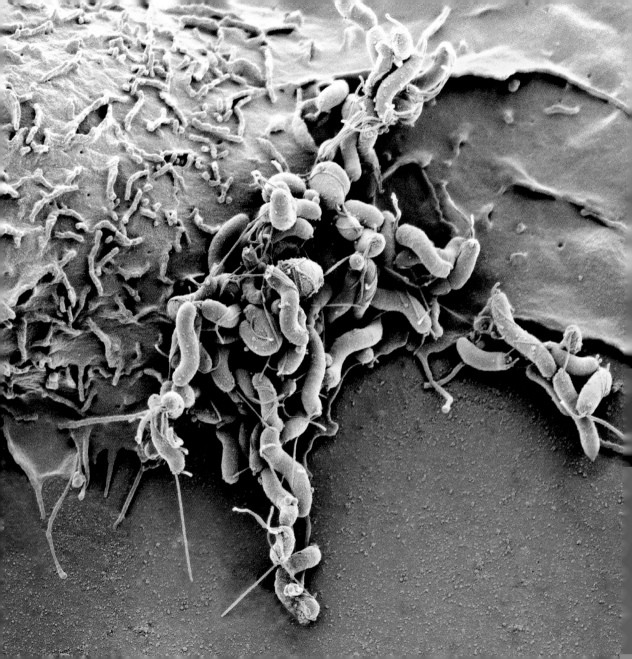

Electron micrograph of *Helicobacter pylori* bacteria (yellow) on human gastric epithelial cells (grey). These spiral-shaped bacteria propel themselves with a whip-like extension, called a flagellum.

barry marshall and robin warren

DR MOHAMED KHADRA

'Half of what you have been taught in medical school will no longer be true in five years. This troubles me, but what troubles me more is that I don't know which half it is.'

– Attributed to C. Sidney Burwell, Dean of Harvard Medical School (1935–1949), in a speech to medical graduates.

'You did what?' exclaimed Adrienne Marshall. 'You drank a broth of bacteria? Are you mad?'

Perhaps Professor Barry Marshall was mad, a mad scientist. However, he and Professor Robin Warren, the Nobel Prize winners for Medicine or Physiology in 2005, were about to overturn the medical community's long-held beliefs about the causation and treatment of one of the most common ailments affecting humanity. Peptic ulcer had acquired a reputation as the disease of the twentieth century, and ten per cent of adults in Western countries had the episodic severe abdominal pain, ulceration of the stomach and duodenum, and the unpredictable life-threatening bleeding or perforation that was part of this disease.

When Marshall was in medical school he had been taught that peptic ulcer disease was caused by too much acid in the stomach and was certainly due to psychic disturbances, such as stress. He was also taught that it was a hereditary disease and, hence, treatment was unlikely to ever cure it. At best doctors could simply control it.

Much of what we had been taught about how the stomach worked dated back to the experiments of Dr William Beaumont on a young man, Alexis St Martin, who was accidentally shot in the stomach in 1833. He survived but continued to have a permanent hole between his stomach and the skin of his abdomen, a fistula. Dr Beaumont, an army surgeon, was able to talk the young man into allowing him to conduct a number of experiments on the physiology of the stomach. This and other experiments had shown that stressful stimuli and the expectation of food increased stomach acid secretion. Some people were hyper-secretors of acid and formed ulcers.

To treat ulcers, you needed to reduce the stomach acid. This was done largely through antacids or surgery. It was not uncommon to operate on patients with ulcer disease during my training and to selectively cut the vagus nerves around the stomach that stimulated acid secretion. It was not until the work of Sir James Black, another Nobel Prize Laureate, in the early 1970s that stomach acid was found to be secreted in response to a type of histamine receptor. The vagus nerve stimulated acid secretion through these receptors. However, normal antihistamines, the type that might be used to turn off the secretions of the nose in a cold, did not work. There had to be another type of histamine receptor, Type 2. He developed an antihistamine that worked specifically to block these receptors and succeeded in reducing stomach acid secretion. Ranitidine (Zantac) and Cimetidine (Tagamet) became commonly used for the treatment of ulcer disease. The problem was that as soon as patients stopped the medication, their ulcers returned.

Since 1979 Professor Robin Warren, a pathologist at the Royal Perth Hospital, had been processing biopsy samples from patients with gastric disease and could not help but notice that a large number contained changes that could only be caused by bacteria. All pathologists around the world must have seen the same changes as they peered into their microscopes daily, and yet it was Warren that challenged the known.

There had been isolated reports in the medical literature as early as the 1890s of pathologists finding bacteria in the stomach – in humans, pigs and dogs. The medical community ignored these early findings; everyone knew 'nothing grows in the highly acidic environment of the stomach'. Professor Warren collected the surgical samples from individuals suffering from gastritis and clearly identified that there were microorganisms, a variant of the type that had been associated with other gastrointestinal infections, such as typhoid.

Professor Warren had completed the first step. It was not until a young trainee physician named Barry Marshall turned up, offering to help with the project, that the research moved forward.

The pair, now a clinico-pathological research team, spent a year trying to isolate the curved bacteria, and each time the laboratory would report back that no microorganisms had grown on the cultures. Step two of Koch's postulates (see below) seemed impossible to prove. This was until Easter Thursday of 1982, when the Royal Perth Hospital was hit with an epidemic of *Staphylococcus aureus*, 'golden staph'. The laboratory technicians were overwhelmed with cultures to process and had no time to look at Marshall's research cultures. When they were finally read on Tuesday, after five days, the new bacteria were seen. Previous cultures had only been read on day two and then discarded when they showed nothing.

Just finding the microorganisms was not enough; Marshall had to satisfy the rigorous methodology laid down in the late 1890s by Robert Koch, who had won the Nobel Prize in 1905. His postulate was that to definitively prove that a microorganism was associated with a disease, one had to show that the microorganism was present in individuals suffering from the disease; isolate the microorganism from a diseased individual and grow it in culture in the laboratory; reproduce the disease when the microorganism is introduced into a healthy individual; isolate the microorganism back out again from the individual thus infected, and show that it is identical to the original microorganism.

All four steps needed to be satisfied before the international medical community was inclined to give any credibility to a theory that overturned one of the 'basic and known facts of medicine' that all of us had been taught in medical school.

Marshall was now working at Fremantle Hospital, where they supported his radical approach to the new ideas. He began to experiment with antibiotic treatments on his willing ulcer patients and found that, not only was he able to cure their ulcers, but they could stop taking all previous medications and remain ulcer free. This new treatment offered a genuine cure, not just a new treatment.

To satisfy the third step of Koch's postulates, Marshall knew what had to be done. He had written about the need for a human subject to be exposed to the bacteria in his thesis plan of 1983. It was unethical to ask anyone else. He had to back his hunch. And so it was that he turned up to the laboratory for his secret experiment. A colleague, Neil Noakes, scraped the heavily infected culture of *Helicobacter pylori* into an alkaline preparation, much like beef broth, and Marshall drank 100ml of the fluid. After ten days of illness, he asked a colleague to endoscope him. There, under the microscope and to his utter delight, were gastric erosions, pus cells and the whole field was teaming with *Helicobacter*. It was only then that Barry told his wife.

This is a uniquely Australian story, one in which the august and unchallenged pronouncements of experts throughout the world were disbelieved and overturned. It is this irreverence, this ability to see rather than to look, that makes Warren and Marshall great. ∎

Director Peter Weir on the set of the film *Picnic at Hanging Rock*. His
1975 classic ushered in a new era of delicacy and skill Australian
film had never seen before.

peter weir and the new australian cinema

DAVID STRATTON

Despite general acceptance that the first feature-length film, i.e. over one hour,
made anywhere in the world was *The Story of the Kelly Gang,* shot in Australia
by Charles Tait in 1906 a full six years before films of a comparable length were
made in America, our cinema has not fared well over the past hundred years. The
pioneering days of silent cinema, roughly until 1929, were tarnished, as Andrew
Pike and Ross Cooper explain in their book *Australian Film 1900–1977,* by a
struggle for power between film distributors and exhibitors (the cinema owners).
The myth that Australian films were 'below standard' and that audiences did not
want to see them prevailed, even as Hollywood, in the wake of World War I,
gained worldwide ascendancy with its powerful star system and international
publicity machine.

      We can no longer assess the vast majority of Australian films made
during this period because most of them were deliberately destroyed; those that
survive, including the work of Raymond Longford (*The Sentimental Bloke, On
Our Selection*), testify to a uniquely Australian approach to the art.

      With ninety per cent of the country's cinemas controlled by American
and British interests, little encouragement was given to local productions, and

once Greater Union ceased to support Ken G. Hall's series of Cinesound features in 1940, the Australian film industry was virtually dead and remained so for a grim thirty years. True, some foreign films were made in Australia during that period: *The Overlanders, The Sundowners, On the Beach* and *Walkabout* are the most famous. Even *Wake in Fright* (1970), regarded by many as the beginning of the Australian New Wave, was a US–Australian co-production, directed by a Canadian.

The revival of the film industry in the early 70s was encouraged by the mood of the time, a mood for change and a desire to replace foreign entertainment, both on television and in cinemas, with local stories and local faces. Lobbyists successfully persuaded the Liberal–Country Party government to support a local industry with cold hard cash. The initial results were populist but not especially distinguished: the *Barry Mackenzie* and *Alvin Purple* comedies attracted large audiences but were never likely to go down in film history as major works.

All that changed in 1975 with the release of Peter Weir's second feature, *Picnic at Hanging Rock*. Like most of the other directors of his generation, Weir had not gone to a film school. He had learnt his craft working on the floor of the ATN 7 television studios in Sydney, had made short films on 16mm and had proved with his innovative, genre-crossing feature debut *The Cars that Ate Paris* (1974) that he was a director with a distinctive approach. It was Patricia Lovell, known to television viewers as the host of *Mr Squiggle*, who brought Joan Lindsay's entirely fictional 1967 book to Weir's attention and who struggled to raise the budget of under $500,000 – minuscule by today's standards but formidable then. (One-third of the budget was federally funded, another third came from the Government of South Australia, and the remainder was provided by the Greater Union.)

This eerie story about the disappearance of a couple of schoolgirls and a teacher while climbing Hanging Rock on St Valentine's Day in 1900 was handled with a delicacy and skill never before seen in this country. Every element of the production was close to perfection: Cliff Green's screenplay, which daringly left the mystery unresolved; Russell Boyd's luminous photography; the eerie panpipe music of Gheorghe Zamfir; the performances of the actors, both adult (Helen Morse, Jacki Weaver, John Jarratt) and adolescent (Anne Lambert, Karen Robson). The critics were (mostly) ecstatic, rightly divining that a new era in local production had dawned, and audiences flocked to see the film which, in a time before the multiplex, ran for months in city cinemas. *Picnic* was sold all over the world and remains one of the most highly regarded of all Australian films, proof positive that it's not necessary to talk down to an audience to find success.

Weir went on to make more important films. *The Last Wave* (1977), which today is more timely than ever it was, is about climate change and an impending apocalypse; *Gallipoli* (1981) remains the best film about Australians at war; *The Year of Living Dangerously* (1982) was a fine adaptation of the Christopher Koch novel about an Australian journalist in Indonesia at the time of an attempted coup. From then on Weir made his films in America, although he never lived there, and brought his own distinctive, very Australian, sensibility to Hollywood productions, without ever compromising his own integrity. *Witness* (1985), *The Mosquito Coast* (1986), *Dead Poets Society* (1989), *Green Card* (1990), *Fearless* (1993), *The Truman Show* (1998) and *Master and Commander* (2003) are all, in very different ways, remarkable films. Weir has not been prolific, but he refuses to settle for second-best and has always insisted on making the films he wants to make as far as possible on his own terms. As a result, he has unprecedented respect in an industry not noted for its respect for artists.

Weir was not the only important figure involved in the Australian New Wave: Fred Schepisi (*The Devil's Playground*, *The Chant of Jimmie Blacksmith*), Bruce Beresford (*Don's Party*, *The Getting of Wisdom*, *Breaker Morant*), Gillian Armstrong (*My Brilliant Career*), Phillip Noyce (*Newsfront*) and George Miller (*Mad Max*) all made major contributions to Australian cinema in the 1970s. For many reasons, Australian films no longer attract the audiences they did then, neither here nor abroad. Perhaps we need a new Peter Weir to raise the banner for quality, intelligence, vision and a distinctively Australian voice. ∎

the smoko

HUMPHREY McQUEEN

'Smoko' means more than the dictionary's definition of 'a rest from work; tea-break'.

The 'smoko' joined the Australian greats as an emblem of the battles by trade unionists against the ten-hour day and a sixty-hour week, and for paid annual holidays and long-service leave.

The idiom of 'smoko' represents our fondness for adding 'o' or 'y' to abbreviated words, such as 'baccy' for tobacco. 'Smoko' came out of 'Smoke-ho!', where 'Ho!' is a cry for attention, as in 'Yo-ho!', a call to knock off at the end of a shift. Recent bans on smoking inside workplaces have redefined 'smoko' as the entitlement that smokers have to slip outside. 'Cuppa' became a domestic form of 'smoko', which referred to a break for some food and a drink.

An English visitor to the Victorian goldfields reported in 1855 on 'a curious practice … of taking a "smoking time" in the forenoon for a quarter of an hour, and again in the afternoon for a quarter of an hour. All the men leave off work and deliberately sit down and smoke.' The term 'smoke oh!' itself was not recorded until 1865.

Why did workers need a smoko? British immigrants complained about the heat and glare as they campaigned for an eight-hour day from 1855. More generally, the pace inside factories, offices and shearing sheds was more relentless than the rhythms of nature that had set the pattern of rural labour. Outback shepherds often had little to do but sit, smoke and go barmy.

The President of the Arbitration Court ruled in 1913 that the 'working time of the labourer is time purchased by the employer, who has the exclusive right to it'. A few months earlier, the micromanagement of work by stopwatches had reminded Australian engineers of 'the whip of owners or taskmasters'.

Experts realised that a smoko improved performance, in quality and quantity. Bosses begrudged smokos because they were paying for the down time. Moreover, they objected because stopping and starting the flow of materials and machinery, even for a few minutes, cost more than the wages.

The right to stop, for how long and under what circumstances sparked disputes. In 1950, a Western Australian award stipulated that a smoko for 'the period of seven minutes shall not be exceeded by any circumstances'. A corporation sacked Sydney workers in 1957 for sitting down during their break. A strike got them reinstated before the supervisor admitted that the sackings had been intended to intimidate the whole workforce into a speed-up.

With sixty per cent of adult males addicted to nicotine in the 1950s, employers had to regulate the need to smoke. Ownership of labour time was the driver here too. Whether workers could smoke on the job and be profitable depended on their tasks and on whether they were being paid by the piece or by the hour. A brickie's labourer explained that 'a pieceworker can smoke, talk or do anything at all, so long as he gets plenty of bricks and mortar'.

In nineteenth-century Australia, plug tobacco was popular because it did not dry out as readily as cut or shag. The plug was so hard that it had to be shaved with a knife, and the chips rolled in the palm of the hand to fill a pipe. This process took up too much time on the job. Hence, men filled a brace of pipes, which they stuck into their bowyangs, or they secured a couple of roll-your-owns behind their ears.

Around 1900, airproof tins kept cut tobacco moist, which brought a shift from pipes to roll-your-owns, a skill with twenty-five movements. Roll-your-owns required papers with a gummed edge to keep the durries together. One brand promoted itself: 'Smoko times are short so I roll a Better cigarette Quicker with ZIG-ZAG.'

In the nineteenth century, the custom was for work to start at 7 am and to stop an hour later for breakfast. As operations became more mechanised, employers allowed only one meal break a day, at noon. Manual workers who started too early to feel like breakfast smoked to ward off hunger pains. They pushed for a morning smoko well before they demanded an afternoon one. Hard yakka on little or no food drove them to gorge on sugars and fats washed down with sweet tea.

Shearing gangs elected and paid for their own cooks, and for their own food. On top of a hearty breakfast, the shearers needed a thirty-minute smoko to replenish their energy. A 1911 account reported 'coffee, cocoa and chocolate or tea, with ham or cheese sandwiches, cakes, scones and pastry'. With shearers paid by the number of fleece shorn, the long breaks cost the squatters nothing.

Supplying potable water to worksites led to another Australian 'great' – the Furphy – the trade name for a cast-iron tank on wheels. A 'furphy' became slang for rumour because workers and soldiers swapped yarns around the water cart. Billy boys and tea ladies also spread gossip.

Because smoko times were so brief, a billy boy or nipper had to maintain a fire so that the tea water was boiling at the start. Later on, individuals relied on thermos flasks while the spread of electricity introduced urns and jugs. During the 1960s, the mass marketing of tea bags, instant coffee and vending machines threatened the tea-break since workers no longer had to stop at the same time.

The 'smoko' remains popular because it provides a chance for making friends. ■

JAMES DIBBLE

A.B.C. NEWS

'aunty' ABC

TIM BOWDEN

At the ripe old age of seventy-seven, 'Aunty' ABC is a feisty old bird who refuses to entertain the thought of drifting quietly into a retirement home. Indeed, she dresses defiantly in purple and rattles her walking stick along the park railings of respectability, frequently taking part in protest rallies to protect the environment or safeguard civil liberties. She has had a personal computer for the last fifteen years, and enthusiastically emails and surfs the internet to stay in contact with her many nieces, nephews and friends across the generations.

Yet who is she, and how did we get her? National public broadcasters are an endangered species in the twenty-first century. When the Australian Broadcasting Commission began broadcasting at 8 pm on Friday 1 July 1932, the chimes of the Sydney General Post Office were carried to twelve radio stations in all Australian states. The ABC was modelled on the British Broadcasting Corporation, which had begun only six years earlier and was expected to bring high culture to the masses – like plays, classical concerts, uplifting talks, church services and educational broadcasts. The BBC's first Director-General, John Reith, a staunch Presbyterian, not only ruled it with a rod of iron but had very firm opinions about what was suitable to be broadcast on the radio. It used to be said that the measure of what could go to air was that it would not offend John Reith's notional maiden aunt!

And yes, like the BBC, early ABC announcers did actually wear dinner jackets in the studio to present the evening radio programs. It took the arrival of television in Britain, and commercial television at that, to take Aunty out of her corsets, thick lisle stockings and sensible shoes. Historian Ken Inglis believes that the term 'Aunty' was in popular currency in the late 1950s when the brash popular appeal of commercial television was such a contrast with the straitlaced BBC that the Beeb was dubbed 'Aunty'.

The term was quickly imported to Australia, although Inglis noted that a writer in *The Bulletin* in 1957 thought the nickname 'more a token of reliability – quality, if you like – than an epithet of ridicule'. Aunty became a term of affection. During one of the ABC's many funding crises – in this case brought about by the Fraser Coalition Government in 1976 – a support group was formed in Melbourne calling itself Aunty's Nephews and Nieces, which later merged with the Friends of the ABC.

Aunty was a skittish twenty-six-year-old when television came to Australia in 1956. The Australian Prime Minister, Sir Robert Menzies, didn't want it and was certainly not prepared to spend large amounts of Commonwealth money on this new medium. The ABC's long-serving and wily General Manager, Sir Charles Moses, simply grafted television onto the Commission's radio structure, blandly assuring the government it wouldn't cost much. Our early television efforts were literally radio with pictures, delivering news, sport, drama, concerts, church services, education programs, documentaries and children's shows like *Playschool*, using the human resources available at the time. Some radio people were good on television, some weren't. However, they were exciting times when producers were given enormous freedom to experiment with this exciting new technical toy. In 1960 producer Ray Menmuir staged a live production of Shakespeare's *Richard II* in prime time from Sydney's two main studios! The 1970s saw an explosion of cheeky new comedy, like *Aunty Jack* and the gormless reporter Norman Gunston. Aunty's image was certainly changing as a mustachioed cross-dresser wearing boxing gloves was now threatening to 'rip your bloody arms off'.

Although *Four Corners* had existed since 1961, nightly current affairs began with *This Day Tonight* in 1967, its cheeky irreverence and tough political interviews enraging the federal government and a timid ABC senior management in equal measure.

I have to confess to being only seven years younger than Aunty, and one of her public faces from 1987 to 1994, when I fronted the viewer reaction program *Backchat*. I thought I had a good face for radio, and so did Sydney television critic Jim Oram when he wrote: '*Backchat*'s forum is astonishingly simple. Its commentator Tim Bowden (who reminds one of a koala and therefore should be protected) sits in front of a camera introducing written comments from the viewers.'

Handling the weekly inflow of letters (yes, people still wrote them then), I was constantly intrigued by the ingenious invective of those who wrote to complain about what they didn't like. One viewer, early in Andrew Denton's television career, snarled, 'Who was on quality control at the ABC the night that little dud crawled out of the primeval slime . . .' There was also a strong underlying affection in the correspondence for Aunty ABC and its role as the national broadcaster. Consumers felt that it was indeed 'their' ABC and, as family members, had the right to have their say. I also got a new take on Aunty in 1989 from G. James, of North Carlton, Victoria: 'Aunty is an independent-minded woman in her sixties who lives in the Dandenongs, wears a parka and inclines towards eating what we weren't meant to eat and believing what we weren't meant to believe.'

Somehow, despite the fury and senseless budget cutting of both Labor and Coalition governments over the years because of alleged political bias (I always find it interesting that the viewers and listeners might complain about all sorts of things but perceived bias is hardly registered on the reaction radar), Aunty continues to flourish doubtless because of this widespread community support. Despite its board being stacked with those seen as ideologically appropriate members by both sides of politics, the ABC manages to soldier on as a potent national force in an increasingly fragmented television and radio industry.

Perhaps this is the best news in a long time for Aunty ABC. With its myriad radio and television transmitters across the country, a flourishing online internet presence, enthusiastic embracing of podcasting and vodcasting, the advent of digital radio and television services may well give Aunty a brave and flourishing new future – providing the spectre of having advertising inflicted on the ABC can be kept at bay.

Certainly the Australian poet A.D. Hope was in upbeat mood about her prospects when he was asked to compose an *Ode to Aunty* for her fiftieth birthday in 1982. The former Argonaut, 'Anthony Inkwell', concluded:

> For though not many of us may
> Live long enough to see the day
> For being a body corporate
> You may expect no mortal date
> And though the clock with ceaseless tick
> Reminds you that you are no chick,
> You're getting on, dear, but don't fret,
> You'll live to be a hundred yet,
> To ride the ether and its waves
> And dance a jig upon our graves. ■

the milk bar

ELIZABETH FARRELLY

It's easy to romanticise the old milk bar, with its quiet, gossipy warmth and scaly, ever-changing skin of advertising posters. Easier still to romanticise a culture that not only celebrates its defeats beside its victories but iconises its corner stores beside its opera houses. Today's cities may be dotted with convenience retail, open 24/7, but the demise of the great Australian milk bar leaves a hole that no quantum of fluoro-lit convenience can fill. Why? What was so special about the milk bar?

The milk bar was personal, for one thing. Even those formally badged Four Square or IGA were scarcely chain stores, in the modern sense, since their proprietors usually lived beside or above the shop and partook of the local community. In some cases, post-war austerity gave the corner store that deathly understocked feel you associate these days with dying country towns. But in many parts of Australia the corner shops were run almost exclusively by Greek and Italian immigrants who imposed their own aesthetic of abundance, even in the face of poverty. Such shops, forerunners of the modern deli, were scouting for Australia's shift from an Anglo-Celtic monoculture. Scented with salami and cinnamon, brimming with European provender, they were a first inkling that there might be more to the reffo than met the eye.

For me, the corner store was less exotic but no less enchanted. It meant running – for no reason other than, well, why walk? – down, literally, to the corner, holding a list in my mother's near-illegible handwriting. The shop smelt of ground coffee and tobacco and yeasted loaves and oranges and freshly printed newspaper. I would breathe deeply on entering then proudly decipher the list – either for Mr Brown, the stern-faced, brylcreemed shopkeeper whose son sat next to me at school, or for Molly, who wore tartan slippers with pom-poms and whom we all loved.

The list would go something like this. 'One packet of Capstan plain, one packet of Rothmans filter-tip. Quarter of a pound of dark kaffir coffee beans (how I savoured that alliteration) and quarter of American. Half a loaf of bread. One packet of razor blades for Dad.' The bread would be broken down the middle to reveal the soft white kissing-crust, the coffee beans scooped and weighed and poured into stiff waxed paper. Then the whole lot would be put on tick and into a paper sack, the bread on top and almost impossible not to pick on the way home.

What does it signify, apart from a regulation nostalgia for one's own childhood? Well, quite a lot really. It was a world where children were still allowed on the streets off-leash, even before they could read running writing. Where neighbours were presumed benign, apart from the occasional crabby dog, and where children were presumed competent to cross roads and negotiate strangers – not to mention dogs – without the intervening parental eye.

It was also a world where people shopped, on the whole, locally and daily; at the corner shop and in the local high street. Where a pre-modern village-mindedness persisted, despite the fact that most people had cars; perhaps because there was usually just one car per family, and that took the breadwinner to work. A world where people didn't all have freezers in the basement or double garages out front; where we hadn't yet been sucked into the ubiquitous ideology of the supermarket, much less the mega-mall.

It was a world, therefore, in which streets still felt both owned and shared, instead of neither. Where shops still had faces and children still roamed the neighbourhood till dark; where the great blank-walled, outsize hypermart (along with outsize houses, children and carbon footprints) was still a thing of the future.

Some of these differences may be more perceptual than real. Statistics show the contemporary suburb to be, on the whole, safer than its mid-century counterpart. It's our feelings, and our expectations, that have changed.

But there are real changes, too. Feminism, for one. Home ownership, for another. The milk bar was only ever sustainable in a world where most mothers were homebodies, and therefore where one salary was enough. Now, that's all changed – driven partly by women's desire to compete but largely by our definition of 'enough'. A world of home theatres and six-car garages, where every child 'needs' his or her own ensuite, was never going to come free. The milk bar is one small part of the price. ◼

nugget coombs

TIM ROWSE

Herbert Cole ('Nugget') Coombs was an economist, and it helps to understand his importance if we recall that it was during his life span (1906–1997) that economics became the most important idiom in which to understand public questions. By isolating and elevating the economic and financial aspect of a widening range of issues, economists have claimed a special intellectual authority in public affairs since the Great Depression.

Coombs was the son of a railway stationmaster in Bridgetown, Western Australia, and a pupil at Perth Modern School. After taking degrees at the University of Western Australia and the London School of Economics, then serving as an economic analyst in the Commonwealth Bank, Coombs first made a distinctive contribution to public policy in his mid thirties. In 1942 he argued that Australia could afford to be less protective of its industries when World War II came to an end – a demand then being made by the United States on all its allies – as long as rich nations would commit to spending their trade surpluses liberally. As a trade policy adviser and negotiator over the following five years, Coombs gave Australia a distinctive voice in the Allies' planning of a new international economic order. He led the delegation that signed Australia into the General Agreement on Tariffs and Trade. Had he wished to continue a career in multilateral economic diplomacy, the nascent UN would have made him one of their top officials.

However, Coombs favoured domestic politics and, though an outward-looking man, he enjoyed the Australian way of life, particularly in its Sydney forms. He accepted Prime Minister Chifley's invitation to be Governor of the Commonwealth Bank in 1949. Since the late 1930s, Coombs had believed that governments could and should secure full employment. As Director-General of Post-war Reconstruction (1942–45), he had helped shape a full employment policy. As the government's senior monetary policy official, and the bank's Keynesian governor, he had to teach Australia's bankers how to moderate their lending policies to avoid turning full employment into rampant inflation.

The duties of governor were not enough for the energetic Coombs. Just before taking up the governorship, Coombs had shared in redesigning the CSIRO, trying to balance its public accountability with its scientific autonomy. His esteem for scientists was part of his wider belief that education and the arts were essential to the formation of a humane society. He involved himself in the foundation (in 1946) and subsequent governing of the Australian National University. He and his brother economists, with whom he had shared diverse advisory duties during the war, were prominent in the leadership of the ANU until the 1970s. In 1954 Coombs campaigned among Australia's corporate and cultural elites to establish the Australian Elizabethan Theatre Trust, a theatrical entrepreneur and grant-giving fund that gradually lured the Commonwealth government into taking responsibility for 'arts policy'. His own tastes in the arts were mildly modernist, but the more anti-humanist elements of modernism left him cold.

In each of these efforts in institutional design – banking, higher education, scientific research, the performing arts – Coombs worked from a strong sense of noblesse oblige. That is, he firmly believed that it was the responsibility of the top people in the public and private sector, and not just of elected politicians, to give constructive and disinterested leadership. Coombs himself was widely welcomed in such circles; if the more conservative members of Australia's elites were sometimes ruffled by his liberal views, they did not close their doors to him. In 1971 *The Australian* made him 'Australian of the Year', and in 1972 Gough

Whitlam enhanced his political appeal when he foreshadowed that, if he became Prime Minister, he would make Coombs his adviser.

By then, Coombs had new causes to advocate. Upon his retirement from the Reserve Bank in 1968, he had become Chair of the Council for Aboriginal Affairs, a position he held until 1976. He quickly learned how resistant Aborigines had become to others' plans to assimilate them. Turning his attention to the economic institutions of northern Australia, including the welfare system into which Aborigines were then being admitted, he advocated adaptations in land tenure, social security and local government that recognised their different aspirations. (In recent policy debate, his schemes have been caricatured as the 'Coombs socialist experiment'.) He found the Yirrkala community especially engaging over many visits from 1968 until the early 1990s, challenging him to spell out the practicalities of 'Aboriginal autonomy'.

Another retirement interest was the human relationship with nature. In 1970 he published one of the earliest papers considering the implications, for economic policy, of the new message from scientists that the human race was exhausting natural resources. He developed a critical interest in the models of 'human nature' that economists had long assumed; and in 1977 he became President of the Australian Conservation Foundation. His conservationism was nurtured by his close friendship with the writer Judith Wright.

Coombs was at ease with Australians' informality, and greatly preferred the nickname 'Nugget' to 'Herbert' (and few got away with calling him 'Bertie'). Three explanations of 'Nugget' evoke something of his personality. He was significantly shorter than the average Australian male, but athletically taut and charmingly direct in his address. Admirers, as his achievements mounted, said that his nickname connoted that he was 'pure gold'. Coombs, who declined Menzies' offer of a knighthood, preferred to explain his name by pointing out that the smallest and strongest beast in a bullock team was known – in bullocky patois – as 'the nugget'. Much of his leadership skill was to find the path of common interest and to make others feel valued in their contribution to it.

Coombs was lecturing in Darwin to a conference on Aboriginal health in October 1995, exploring ways that social welfare payments could be channelled into activities directed by women in remote Aboriginal communities, when he suffered the stroke that terminated his active life. From 1931, as President of the UWA Students Union, to Visiting Fellow at the ANU, he spent 64 years applying the disciplines of economic thought to humane ends. Unique in the length and energy of his public service, it was Coombs' particular genius to imagine the governmental mechanisms in which to pursue social ideals. ∎

judith wright

VERONICA BRADY

Judith Wright, some say, is a national treasure. If so, she is a feisty one, born into a distinguished pastoral family but a passionate advocate of justice for Aboriginal people and friend of Oodgeroo Noonuccal (Kath Walker), poet, critic, environmentalist, feminist and general activist. At the height of World War II, when Japanese invasion seemed imminent, her first poems appeared, affirming her love of the land – 'my blood's country' – and her pride in stories of pioneering courage, loneliness and endurance. But she also turned the tradition inwards and invoked a new 'feminine' dimension, seeing the land, as her *Preoccupations in Australian Poetry* put it, as the outer equivalent of an inner reality and which, as 'Nameless Flower' suggests, she felt responsible somehow to put into words:

Flakes that drop at the flight of a bird and have no name,
I'll set a word upon a word to be your name.

This points the sense of self inwards, but to a more intense relationship between the psychic and the physical as her second collection celebrates the mysteries of pregnancy and birth, love and tenderness but also an intimate sense of the interconnectedness of all life. Growing up on the family property 'in very close contact with a large and splendid landscape', she had always felt herself 'a good deal smaller than just I' so that the land became a living presence, something that ran through the blood.

From early on this set her in conflict with what she called 'the "I tradition" – the ego, it's me and what I think', which was responsible for a culture of '"mechanised stupidity, mechanised falsity and mechanised self-destruction" which she believed threatened the continuing existence of human truth, and . . . the survival of the human world'.

So throughout her life she was a passionate environmentalist, leading the battle to save the Great Barrier Reef and the rainforests in the 1970s and, at the other end of the scale, participating in the inquiry into the National Estate set up by the Whitlam government. But the land also spoke to her of the Aboriginal past, of a 'tribal story/ lost in [the] alien tale' we had brought here from the other side of the world. The fact that her father had had an Aboriginal nurse probably meant that she heard from him stories from the other side of the frontier, like the early massacre of local Aborigines driven over a cliff near the family property for spearing their sheep and cattle, which is the subject of 'Nigger's Leap, New England'. Its realisation that 'the black dust our crops ate' was *their* dust and that 'all men are one man at last' was unusual in the 1940s when it was written, and may still be provocative today.

Similarly, her family history, *The Generations of Men,* interrogated the pioneering legend, declaring that the settlers had spoken 'words of power but not words of life' and the fate of Aboriginal Australia means that our 'whole civilization' is like a 'house haunted by the ghost of a dead man buried under it'. Until we come to terms with this, our 'every achievement [will be] empty and every struggle vain'. As time went on, her friendship with Aboriginal writers and activists like Oodgeroo Noonuccal and Kevin Gilbert made her aware of the ways in which indigenous suffering continues, and she became a champion of their struggle for recognition and justice. In the 1980s, with the distinguished public servant 'Nugget' Coombs, she campaigned for a treaty with Aboriginal Australia, and her last public action only a week or so before her death was to lead the Reconciliation Bridge Walk in Canberra.

But she was no sentimentalist. She and her husband, Jack McKinney, were very interested in contemporary philosophy and science, especially in quantum physics and its sense of the importance of what she called 'reasons beyond the reach of reason' and feeling for the interrelatedness of all life. Her awareness of the interplay between the observer and the observed, inner and outer reality, increased her respect for Aboriginal culture as well as for the natural world and underlay her opposition to war in general and to nuclear weapons in particular.

Wright was an original and prophetic thinker prepared to face the truth and explore new possibilities in a comfortable, complacent society. She also had the intelligence and courage to realise that, to quote from the poem which concludes her *Collected Poems*, 'the dark itself [may be] the source of meaning', that we need to extend the range of commonsense and speak more respectfully of what is unseen – as contemporary science does – and continue the search for order in an enigmatic universe. As a society, we might follow Judith Wright beyond ego, division and concreteness into the underlying commonalities that make true humanity possible. ∎

nancy wake

SARAH MACDONALD

World War II was a calamity, but it was the making of Nancy Wake. A woman with a personality perhaps too constrained by peacetime, this adventurer began the conflict a hedonistic socialite and ended it a hero of the Resistance. While she was not immune to the war's horror, Wake's spirit still managed to shine strongly in a time of darkness.

With her Kiwi blood, British allegiance and French soul often rising to the fore, Nancy has always had a troubled relationship with Australia. Yet, her character shines with attributes we like to claim as our own – an aptitude for bullshitting, a brilliant ability to drink and a healthy disrespect for authority. These traits showed up early – at sixteen, Nancy felt so suffocated by life on the 'insular peninsula' of Sydney's Neutral Bay that she ran away from home. Four years later she fooled her family doctor into helping her acquire a passport and then, in England, tricked a newspaper recruiter into believing she knew Egyptian hieroglyphics. This set her up as a correspondent in the place she most longed to live: Paris.

Those were heady days, and Nancy was a party animal of the highest calibre and strongest stamina. In 1936 she met her match in Marseilles playboy Henri Fioca; the wealthy industrialist's family wasn't thrilled about the interloper from the Antipodes, so the bride spiked the punch to ensure no one spoilt her wedding party. Nancy loved easily and made friends everywhere, but it was her hatred of injustice and oppression that transformed her life. After witnessing Nazi soldiers terrorise Jews in Vienna and Hitler rally Berliners, she resolved to do whatever she could to stop Fascism.

Nancy Wake was in Britain when war was declared, but her offer to help was met with a suggestion of canteen duties. Tea and bickies were definitely not this dame's forte so she returned to France thinking, as she put it, 'to hell with the consequences'. Over the next few years she deliberately cultivated the image of a gorgeous, giddy goodtime girl; lunching in the right places, promenading in Coco Chanel and even flirting with Nazi soldiers while really working as a courier to the French Resistance, helping more than one thousand Jews escape.

In 1943 the Gestapo began to close in on the woman they called the 'white mouse'; Nancy faked a casual 'back soon' to her beloved Henri and attempted escape. After capture, a daring rescue by the Resistance, a scrub for scabies and a tumble from a moving train, she walked over the Pyrenees in a blizzard, only to be thrown in a Spanish jail.

Back in Britain, the mouse refused to scurry to safety, instead training for the Special Operations Executive with a mission to return to France. Ever the practical joker and always one of the boys, Nancy broke into her official file to read that she'd passed her test despite attaching condoms to her instructor's clothes and hoisting his pants up a flagpole.

On 29 April 1944, Nancy parachuted into the Auvergne region of central France, concealing silk stockings, high heels and a cyanide tablet beneath her overalls and a hangover behind her gasmask. She became 'Madame Andrée', spending the rest of the war living among two hundred Maquis in rough mountain camps. Nancy mostly organised supply drops, distributed weapons and maintained radio contact with the UK but occasionally joined in sabotage raids – scaling bridges with explosives roped around her waist, throwing a grenade into the local Gestapo headquarters and killing a Nazi sentry with her bare hands. Nancy believes her proudest achievement was cycling 500 kilometres in 72 hours through German checkpoints to send a vital message to London.

Nancy Wake adored the daring life and the camaraderie with the Maquis. While she could lock horns with anyone she thought was stuck up, most of her comrades respected her toughness and loved her joie de vivre. After a night of drinking them under the table, Nancy would then remove her make-up and slip on a frilly nightie to sleep. Resistance leader Henri Tardivat described his comrade as 'the most feminine woman I know, until the fighting starts. Then she is like five men.'

The end of the war brought devastation with the discovery that Henri had been tortured and killed by the Gestapo for refusing to give her away. Victory parades and reunions aside, Wake felt so uncharacteristically depressed and bored that she drifted back to Australia. Here she made what she calls her biggest mistake – joining the Liberal Party. Wake had always given politics short shrift and felt used for her war record, while her refusal to wear stockings and a hat upset some party faithful. Nancy was glad she didn't win a seat – she would have struggled to toe the party line, but our parliament probably missed out on a terrific verbal bomb-thrower.

After remarrying, Nancy spent much of her middle age back in Australia, but now lives in her element among other war heroes in a retirement home in Britain. By all accounts she still likes a drink, an argument and stirring the pot. The former white mouse has said she wants her ashes scattered over the French mountains, where she lived life the way she loved it – large and on the edge. ∎

bachelor & spinster balls

RACHAEL TREASURE

In my youth I've travelled from Bothwell to Bathurst, from Dubbo to Deniliquin, on a crawl of Bachelor & Spinster Balls. I was a rum-thirsty girl in a Toyota Corona with a roo bar on the front, stickers on the back and a bodgy muffler. Dirt roads, cattle grids and thousands of k's never put me off.

So why would a young girl travel so far and spend what would have amounted to a house deposit on country partying? It wasn't because I was desperate and dateless . . . it was because of the rush that comes from the uniquely rural, uniquely Australian event that is the B&S.

So come with me, dear reader, chuck your swag on the ute, throw a square-bear of Bundy Rum and a box of Barbecue Shapes in the esky, let them swim together as the ice melts, and I'll take you into my world of B&S Balls.

If you're a bloke, you'll need an op-shop dinner suit and a not-so-white shirt. Brown boots will suffice, and certainly bring a black tie. If you're a chick, a dress from the previous decade will do, and leave the heels at home unless you want them trashed and forever holding the stench of sheep manure. Bring your Blunnie boots, but leave the airs and graces at home.

B&S Balls are as pure as they are dirty. They're as politically incorrect as they are accepting of all. They're peaceful yet wild. There's no techno doof-doof music, no sophistication that stifles, no rave-style designer drugs. There's no chardonnays or lattes. Just plenty of beer and Bundy, meat in bread with mayo and dead horse.

On the surface a B&S may look like a piss-drinking, ute-revving party for country yobbos. You may find blokes who will slap some roadkill on the barbie next to the snags for a laugh. And yes, there are sheilas who skol rum straight from their boot and snog fellas on paddocks scattered with sheep ball bearings. But beneath the surface of these wild weekend-long country parties, lies something much more complex – something spiritually significant that needs to be understood.

As American culture swamps our politics, televisions and towns, rural people are clinging to what remains of the pureness of Australian country communities that love, share, laugh and cry together.

The B&S is a place where country people gather to not just party till they drop, but to celebrate our rural culture that holds this country's richest, most intelligent humour and literally feeds our nation. A B&S says to us we are alive and well with proud youth – despite what the media says about rural decline and drought.

A new wave of B&S popularity is surging thanks to the savvy youngsters who have created sites on the internet that host B&S calendars, surveys, survival tips and chat rooms. One top tip I learnt from Becky G on the net was a swag is 'pretty essential, but best if you go back to his 'cause then you don't have to roll it up in the morning'.

When I've danced in the moonlight to Lee Kernaghan's 'There Ain't Nothin Like a Country Crowd', me and the girls are bonded close because we're coarse, we're country and we like it that way. We know that when it rains and when government policy allows, we simply want to grow good food for the world on land we love and care for – and you can't get a life-long goal more important and spiritual than that!

The B&S symbolises everything great about country life. There's the committee members, usually in their twenties, learning all the skills needed to be good community leaders. These young'uns aren't in their bedrooms on PlayStation. They're sorting out insurance, catering, grog orders, security, logistics, sponsorship and promotion.

The B&S Ball is all about charity too. At Charleville's Bulldust & Bowties B&S profits are donated to the Royal Flying Doctor Service. Tassie's Rural Youth Organisation run The Bulllight Bash B&S at the end of Agfest, which is Tasmania's largest single rural field day. These three days annually generate millions for the state, and it is an event created solely by Rural Youth.

A B&S also provides the sharing of solutions between young farmers yarning around the beer keg: how to get the livestock through another failed season and what the latest technology is to further their farms.

The love-matches, too, at a B&S are genuine with no pretence. Only a country girl could find a wobbly-booted bloke, with skin painted the colour of Shrek by food dye, attractive. And when she reads the texta scrawled over his shirt reading, 'Rye Grass Staggers' and he lurches sideways, she gets the joke. A country boy may eye off the expensive-looking city girls, all wispy slim and glam, but at the end of the night he's going for the girl that can down a sixpack with him at the end of a hard day. He's after a country girl with curves that will allow her to throw a sheep on the ute when it's cast and keep him warm in the winter when the sun barely gets above the hill.

The B&S is a place where old country values like helping others and sharing are cherished and spread – be it helping drunk buggers out of the ditch or sharing your swag with a bloke who can't find his. Mateship between both men and women – it's all there in the heart of it. Just don't forget the Berocca. ■

Tom Curnow

G. RICHARDS   PHOTO.   BALLARAT

as game as
tom curnow

GEOFFREY ROBERTSON

Imagine yourself a young country schoolteacher, taking your wife and baby for a Sunday drive. Outside the local pub you are bailed up by a gang of terrorists, and held captive while they plan an atrocity. They are going to derail a train and then shoot any survivors of the crash. You make the terrorists believe that you sympathise with their cause so they allow you to leave with your family, whom they threaten to kill if you do anything to foil their dastardly plot. As darkness falls, you hear the train whistle in the distance. You could leave your home to warn the driver, but your hysterical wife and weeping sister beg you to stay put, and not to risk their lives, your life and that of your child. What do you do?

True heroism must pass two tests of time – historical time (will the nobility of the cause still be recognised in the future?) and actual time (was there long enough for reflection and for a genuine choice of the heroic course of action?). The dividing line between greatness and foolhardiness may be a nanosecond, with the outcome decided by luck, but people worth celebrating as exemplars always make choices that are informed by a clear-eyed appreciation of the consequences. They are prepared to risk the sacrifice of themselves, and/ or their loved ones, to serve a greater human good, and, unlike self-regarding jihadists and other martyrs, expect nothing in return – in this life or after it.

A nation that does not honour its heroes condemns itself to an undistinguished future. So how come Australians have never heard of Tom Curnow?

He was that young schoolteacher in Glenrowan in 1880, who risked his life when 'Jihad Ned' Kelly rode into town with the blood of three policemen and a police informer fresh upon him. At gunpoint, the Kelly gang forced railway workers to pull up the rail tracks and the stationmaster to give information about the special train, with police and blacktrackers aboard, that had been sent from Melbourne.

Of all the townsfolk held hostage at the pub, only the clever, calculating and utterly courageous schoolmaster proved capable of doing the right thing. He pretended sympathy with the gang, giving them advice and even dancing a jig with the disgusting Dan Kelly, whilst the outlaws boasted of how they would kill the civilians as well as police if they were on the doomed train. Curnow tricked them into allowing him to take his family home before dark. There, heedless of tearful pleas from wife and sister, on hearing the whistle of the approaching train he set off to walk up the track, holding aloft his sister's red shawl in front of a lighted candle. This makeshift warning signal caused the engine driver to stop, whereupon the teacher told him of the murderous trap that lay a short distance ahead. The rest is history – Australian history, at least.

Thomas Curnow had every reason to expect vengeance – the Kellys repeatedly threatened to kill anyone who helped the police. Perhaps if he *had* been gunned down, as these murderous thugs had recently gunned down police informant Aaron Sherritt, he might have been noticed and even applauded by the later generations who were to idealise and iconise Ned Kelly. Instead, Curnow has disappeared down history's memory hole, no more than a trivia quiz question that nobody (not even Barry Jones) answers correctly. In fleeting appearances in films and plays about the siege at Glenrowan, Curnow is depicted as an ugly, elderly pedant, a caricature dobber-inner of these likeable, misunderstood Irish larrikins.

The real Tom Curnow was handsome – 25 at the time – although he walked with a limp from a dislocated hip. After his heroic action at Glenrowan he had to be posted to Melbourne to avoid reprisals from the extended Kelly family and their thuggish friends – a measure of how bushranging had morally corrupted the bush. Curnow's later life was useful and uneventful – he taught until retirement at 60, fathering two sons who came to grief at Gallipoli: one killed, the other severely wounded.

Tom Curnow was an ordinary, decent person who did the right thing at the right time, preventing the mass murder of strangers at the risk of his own and his family's life. None of the other townspeople dared to lift a finger, whilst the railway workers and the stationmaster, albeit at gunpoint, became accomplices to the attempted atrocity. No doubt the Kellys had grievances – some police were corrupt and the jail sentence on Kelly's mother for attacking one such constable was overly harsh – but this cannot begin to excuse her son's bloodthirsty rampage. There is no excuse, either, for Kelly hagiography. At least Nolan's bushrangers inhabit a morally primitive landscape, although Peter Carey wrings a kind of maudlin sympathy for Ned. But the transcript of his trial reveals nothing out of the ordinary about this vicious, reckless criminal. The Jerilderie letter, which inspired Carey, was written by Joe Byrne. Ned's wheedling, lying petition to the Governor for mercy, like his other reported utterances – 'Such is life' is a pretty stupid remark to your executioners – is banal.

Tom Curnow was an ordinary person every day of his life except that momentous Sunday night when his moral sense impelled him to extraordinary action. His bravery may make more sense to us today, when every news bulletin reports some terrorist outrage and even fridge magnets urge us to turn police informer, albeit through the safety of an anonymous hotline.

Ned Kelly is absurd as a national figure. Some day, when Australians come to recognise the cruelty of the man with the upturned bucket on his head, they may allow a fresh hero to emerge from the ashes of the Glenrowan Hotel. A man whom children will compare to others they admiringly describe as being 'as game as Tom Curnow'. ■

the meat pie

MAGGIE BEER

I suspect there are hardly any Australians who have this humble item on their list of the 1001 things to eat before they die. Given that we consume nearly 300 million meat pies a year, few people could be left hankering for their virgin experience.

Having to confess, without any embarrassment, to an elitist view of what the meat pie could be, I thought I'd better do some reading to gather other thoughts on the steamy matter at hand. The first recorded mention of the famed/infamous meat pie I came across was in the Melbourne *Argus* in 1850, which reported that the councillors preferred a meat pie from the pub opposite rather than the food provided in chambers. I suspect in many areas it might be the same today. Another historical footnote leads us to the eccentric Flying Pieman, who, along with engaging in marathon footraces against ferries, sold pies to the crowds at Circular Quay in the mid-1800s. He was certainly part of the early lore we have surrounding our meat pie obsession. So, though pies might have arrived with the British, we certainly took it a step further: tomato sauce, for one. First processed commercially in the early preserving factories around 1868, the meat pie with sauce became the true Australian thing.

There is no doubt it was our first fast food, our answer to America's hot dog. It was the workers' lunch – a meal-in-one, easily managed and quickly eaten. As Michael Symons observes in *One Continuous Picnic*, 'a slow eater was a slow worker' and not to be tolerated. But, damning as I might be about it being such an important part of our Australian cuisine, I have to ask: who has not been tempted by the smell of a hot pie on a cold afternoon at a football match? But I put forward that it's the aroma of the *pastry* that so often tantalises, rather than what's inside. So while I am in constant amazement over why we missed the great opportunities of working with our climate and embracing the Indigenous food culture, rather than slavishly following the habits of the British, a pie with sauce grew to be such a part of our psyche that around the time of World War II it was coined as our 'national dish'.

Even though it might have been a little misdirected, what a pity we didn't listen to Australia's first cookbook. Written in 1864 by Australian Aristologist Edward Abbott, the volume quotes a medical opinion on the 'danger of the meat pie', which warned against not leaving a hole in the crust to let out poisonous gases. The full title of the book was *The English and Australian Cookery Book: Cookery for the Many as well as the 'Upper Ten Thousand'* and, though I've only read summaries of it, Abbott clearly had a wonderful food life, embracing the wild food at hand along with that farmed and cultivated fare, cooked in a sophisticated way. It could still be a lesson for us today.

On another historical note, I've long been an admirer of Dr Philip Muskett, who in 1893 wrote *The Art of Eating in Australia,* which was dedicated to 'the People of Australia with one abiding hope for the development of all the great natural food industries of our Country!' While he didn't write about the meat pie specifically, as far as I know, he did note that at the time we were the biggest meat eaters in the world. In pondering our lack of a national dish, he first thought of damper and tea, yet felt that 'if there was to be one food to meet favour as a national dish, it should surely be the salad'. Muskett eloquently urged us to work with our climate and talked of the struggle between our Anglo-Saxon heritage and our environment. And finally this is happening.

But given that I've confessed to a love of the aroma of freshly cooked pastry, here's one story of how wonderful a pie can be on a cold winter's day with a glass or two of shiraz to wash it down.

The late Maurice de Rohan, who was Agent General for South Australia in London when I first met him, asked me to prepare a cocktail party for over 700 people in Paris in 2001. It was to be held at the Australian Embassy to commemorate the 200th anniversary of Nicolas Baudin's expedition to the southern Australian coast. Maurice gave me free rein to make this a totally South Australian gastronomic event, and so with the help of the team in Paris I managed to fly in an amazing array of ingredients. I was determined this was not going to be just standard cocktail food – I wanted to push some boundaries here. Based on the premise that if Matthew Flinders hadn't pipped Baudin at the post by just five nautical miles at Encounter Bay we might have been French, the concept was to feature the wild food that Baudin found on his journeys around Tasmania into southern Australia.

Maurice immediately loved my idea of whole Murray cods wrapped in mud as if they'd been cooked in coals by the side of the river, traditional damper served with dukkah and our own extra virgin olive oil, oysters from Coffin Bay, yabbies, razor fish, blue swimmer crabs . . . But of course we had to have the meat pie. So for me it was kangaroo tail – first cooked long and slow in Barossa shiraz, shallots and fresh herbs – the meat taken from the bone with loads of the juices reduced to an unctuous glaze and then formed into tiny cocktail pies using a suet pastry. To me, a truly Australian meat pie! ■

mardi gras

CARLOTTA

Having been a part of the Australian entertainment business for over five decades, first appearing at Les Girls Kings Cross in 1963, I know first-hand that being your true self in public doesn't always come easily. You wouldn't know it now that my award-winning *Priscilla Show* is a roaring success, featuring lavish costumes and fabulously expensive sets. Dressing up in drag in the sixties fell under the law of offensive behaviour. I was once arrested and tried to reason with the judge, saying, 'You've got a wig and a robe on, what's the difference?' I must have got him on a good day, because he laughed his head off and said, 'Case dismissed.'

As the words of that famous song goes, 'I've been everywhere, man'. But looking back now, as an icon of the drag scene, it's amazing to see how another Australian icon helped propel and celebrate the issues and lifestyles of our gay and lesbian community. Sydney's Mardi Gras, with the slogan 'Our Freedom, Your Freedom', started in 1978 as the Gay March in Darlinghurst, and aimed at gaining equality and acceptance – both legally and morally – in what was then called the 'normal world'.

As the police arrived to break up the march, violence, bashings and arrests of gays and lesbians, innocently protesting their right to live and love in peace, broke out. But they stood tall and proud, surviving to hold a celebration every year at the same time to remind the rest of Australia that they were still 'out and proud'.

Mardi Gras has come a long way since that first rally thirty years ago, turning into one of the most colourful – and revenue-generating – public events on the Australian calendar. But Mardi Gras is more than just a parade, it's a month-long celebration of theatre, festivals, parties and much, much more. The event attracts thousands of overseas tourists each year and is recognised the world over as an example of tolerance and love over predjudice. The parade alone draws hundreds of thousands of spectators and participants from all walks of life: lesbians, gays, politicians, and families and friends of gays, who proudly exclaim, 'We love our friends and children unconditionally.' Even the police now march alongside the people they arrested all those years ago. This image of community is worth a thousand words.

The streets come alight with the procession of elaborately decorated floats, costumes and wigs that take months to organise and design, masterpieces made lovingly by behind-the-scenes artists and dressmakers working overtime all year round.

Some of the more memorable results have been political satire, like the year when the papier-mâché heads of Fred Nile and Pauline Hanson, vocal opponents of Mardi Gras, bobbled up the street. These send-ups march alongside the more soul-searching floats that campaign for the fight against AIDS, with thousands of helpers along the entire route collecting donations to help fund medical research in their search for a cure.

And Mardi Gras would not be Mardi Gras without the roar of the renowned 'Dykes on Bykes' – hundreds of beautiful lesbians dripping in leather on the backs of the most divine motorcycles you have ever seen. The sound of their horns screaming up the parade route kicks off the festivites, and gives you goosebumps, every year.

The parade passes up Oxford Street and through to the entertainment quarter at Fox Studios, where the legendary after-party is held. People dance all night, socialise and celebrate in many different halls to many different types of music. There is a costume parade where prizes are given out for the best costumes and floats. And during the course of the party there are spectacular shows where everyone from Kylie Minogue, Tina Arena, Chaka Khan and Jimmy Sommerville have performed. The party continues till daylight, when those still standing keep celebrating along Oxford Street all day. I have been part of the parade and party on many occasions and can remember soaking my feet in buckets of water after walking the parade in heels – only to put on another pair of shoes to go to the party.

Mardi Gras is a credit to its past and present presidents, who have maintained the event through good and bad times, and even to people like the Lord Mayor of Sydney, Clover Moore, who makes sure that the celebration doesn't sit in the cultural fringes. One of the great things I admire most about Mardi Gras is the community members who are still militant about their rights in society and each year fight for their respective causes, holding their banners high, proclaiming their beliefs to the spectators.

I truly hope that the government always stands by this wonderful Australian institution that is Mardi Gras and helps it battle through any storms that might come its way. Mardi Gras has changed the attitude of many Australians over the years towards lesbians and gays, by bringing together a greater acceptance and understanding. I have always believed that this event has given a political voice to our community, showing the world that we belong. Like that old song croons, 'There's no business like show business.' And this is the biggest and best show we have. ∎

sir macfarlane burnet

BARRY JONES

Ironically, the greatest scientist Australia ever produced, and whose important work was carried out in Melbourne, is – twenty-three years after his death – barely remembered in his native land. This should be a cause for national shame. The Macfarlane Burnet Institute for Public Health and Medical Research, in Melbourne, commemorates his work, but no other public institution is named for him, not even a Federal electorate, and he is yet to appear on a coin or banknote.

No other Australian medical scientist ever received so many awards for work carried out in Australia. Burnet received the Lasker Award in 1952, the Order of Merit in 1958, the Royal Society's Copley Medal in 1959 and shared the Nobel Prize for Medicine in 1960 with Peter Medawar for their work on 'acquired immunological tolerance'. Three times a knight (Knight Bachelor, KBE, AK), he became the first recipient of the Australian of the Year award in 1961, and was President of the Australian Academy of Science from 1965 to 1969.

There was a somewhat tense rivalry between Burnet and Howard Florey, the developer of penicillin. Florey was born in Adelaide in 1898, but chose to live and work in England from 1922. They shared the triple crown of the Nobel, Copley and OM.

Frank Macfarlane Burnet was born on 3 September 1899 in Traralgon, Gippsland, son of a Scottish-born bank manager, and grew up in Terang. Educated at Geelong College and Melbourne University, he was one of four eminent scientists, all born in the same year and living in Melbourne; they became lifelong friends. The others were Sir Ian Clunies Ross, veterinarian and the charismatic head of CSIRO; Dame Jean Macnamara, who worked heroically in the 1930s treating polio victims in Melbourne and the bush and crusaded for the introduction of myxomatosis to control the rabbit plague; and Sir Ian Wark, metallurgist and educational administrator.

Mac Burnet retained a deep memory of the influenza pandemic that swept the world in 1918 and 1919 and probably killed more people than World War I, and he worked on influenza for 25 years.

Burnet worked in London at the Lister Institute from 1925 to 1927 and the National Institute of Medical Research from 1932 to 1933. He became assistant director of the Walter and Eliza Hall Institute for Medical Research (WEHI) in Melbourne in 1928, and director in 1944, also holding the Melbourne University's chair of Experimental Medicine. In 1944 he declined a glittering offer of a Harvard chair, determined to remain in Melbourne. In 1965 he was succeeded by his protégé, Sir Gustav Nossal, a groundbreaking immunologist who would go on to win Australian of the Year in 2000.

Between 1924 and 1983 he published 528 papers. Burnet, essentially an old-fashioned, solitary, intuitive researcher, was rather suspicious of 'big science', heavy investment in equipment and setting up research teams, and wary of clinical or applied research. His scientific hero was Charles Darwin.

Mac Burnet was a biologist of the old generalist school. He was incorrigibly curious about the mechanism of every natural phenomenon he encountered. His rare gift was to take apparently unconnected observations and fit them into whatever theoretical framework was his current obsession. A particular finding in the classical reductionist mode of normal scientific inquiry – increasingly narrow and specialised – became for Burnet the starting point for broad speculation on the whole nature of life. His experimental work on polio and influenza viruses, assisted by the use of electron microscopes after 1939, resulted in major discoveries about their nature and replication.

Burnet's experiments had extraordinary reach, shaped by extensive reading and deep philosophical reflection. He liked to picture himself as a twentieth-century Erasmus, a prophet in his own land, the scholar and scientific humanist who could remain unattached.

His greatest scientific achievements were theoretical: the concept of 'acquired immunological tolerance' which underpins organ transplantation and skin grafts and the 'clonal selection' theory, a micro-evolutionary explanation of the adaptive nature of antibody production. Both proved to be cornerstones of our understanding of the immune process.

Burnet worked with Frank Fenner on acquired immunological tolerance, the capacity of organisms to distinguish between 'self' and 'not self', which was confirmed experimentally in England by Medawar and Rupert Billingham. Burnet and Medawar received the Nobel Prize for this work. Fenner and Billingham were very unlucky not to have shared the award, because Nobel Prizes can be split into two or three awards, but not four.

In 1955 the Danish medical scientist Niels K. Jerne published a paper on natural selection in cell production. Burnet recognised a basic flaw in the theory, renamed it 'clonal selection', and modified it radically in 1957 arguing, along Darwinian lines, the need for a receptor that selected a few cells from a very large library, making use of pre-existing mutations favoured for multiplication and survival. Burnet advanced the now generally accepted explanation of how the immune system reacts to infection, with both long-term and short-term responses.

Experiments by Gus Nossal and Joshua Lederberg provided formal proof of clonal selection, the theory Burnet regarded as his greatest achievement.

Jerne, who received a Nobel Prize in 1984, wrote, 'I hit the nail, but Burnet hit the nail on its head.'

Burnet died of cancer at his son's home in Port Fairy on 31 August 1985, aged almost 86, and was buried at Tower Hill. His tombstone quotes Plato's words on Socrates: 'A man who threw off ideas like sparks which caused a blaze that leapt across to the minds of others'. ■

"The Leader"   "The Herald"   "The Age"
"The Argus"   "Daily Telegraph"

the proprietors: packer & murdoch

DAVID SALTER

When it comes to securing a venerated place in history, our media proprietors enjoy a unique advantage: they publish the first draft of that history, and set its tone.

Rupert Murdoch owns more than 70 per cent of the newspapers Australians buy every day, and his editors – who rely on him for their jobs – are unlikely to print material that takes serious issue with his character or business ethics. This allows the description of Murdoch as 'a great Australian proprietor' to pass unchallenged, despite Rupert renouncing the citizenship of his birth many years ago to circumvent media ownership restrictions under US law.

When the late Kerry Packer's empire was at its peak, it commanded close to 40 per cent of the national television audience and dominated the women's magazine market. None of those outlets was ever bashful about praising his qualities as a 'great Australian' or celebrating his touch for 'what the ordinary bloke wants'. At the memorial service for Packer (paid for by the taxpayer even though Kerry himself was proud to have contributed virtually no income tax to the nation's treasury throughout his life), the then Prime Minister, John Howard, echoed those obsequious appellations without irony or qualification.

But 'great' is a multi-layered adjective. Packer and Murdoch have undeniably been highly successful and influential media businessmen. But were they truly 'great' in the sense of being elevated and distinguished, or of extraordinary or remarkable ability and achievement? Their greatness is better defined by an older meaning of the word: 'eminent by reason of birth, wealth or power'.

And therein lies the first crucial component of the persuasive mythology the Australian media have been allowed to embroider around their two most dominant proprietors. For decades we've been led to believe that Packer and Murdoch rose to their eminence and wealth from humble beginnings. The truth is that both men were born rich, and with their feet already firmly placed on the ladder of media moguldum. Murdoch inherited a daily newspaper and considerable assets, while Packer inherited a half share in a daily newspaper, two television stations and the most profitable magazine publishing group in the country. They did not work their way up from the mail room to the managing director's office: they started there.

Both young proprietors had obvious talent for the family trade and quickly outstripped the wealth and power of their fathers. Throughout the thirty-five years he controlled the CPH and PBL empires, Packer was repeatedly lauded for his 'passion' for the media industry and abiding personal 'love' of television and the Nine Network he owned. So strong and deep was this affection that when Alan Bond offered him an attractive price for Nine, Packer sold it to him that day without a second thought. The personal loyalty of his staff and thirty-year family connection with the network meant nothing.

Murdoch rarely sells a significant media asset, but he hardly ever creates one. (*The Australian* is the one obvious exception – a credit to Rupert's long-term determination to prove there was a niche for a quality national broadsheet in Australia.) Murdoch's career has been one of aggressive acquisitions, not creations. Many of these purchases weren't to build new assets but simply to liquidate his opposition. Repeatedly hailed as a 'great newspaperman', Murdoch has closed down more newspapers than he ever founded. He then uses the brute force of monopoly capitalism to gouge increased profits from the one-newspaper towns and cities he's fashioned. Advertising revenue is always the measure of News Limited performance, not the quality of its journalism.

For those who have tried to stand in the way of Packer and Murdoch, these two giants of the Australian media have been 'great' proprietors in the same sense that Attila was a 'great' Hun. In the 1970s, Packer attempted to hijack test cricket by secretly signing up the best players. This was his bullying response after the Australian Cricket Board declined to renege on their existing television rights agreement with the ABC. Pressed by a London barrister during the legal battle that followed, Packer freely admitted that his sole motivation for this act of piracy was to make money, not any altruistic desire to secure better pay and conditions for the players.

When Murdoch's datacasting ambitions were thwarted in 2001 by muddled Coalition policy, every News Limited outlet in Australia gave John Howard and his Communications Minister a fearful 'digitorial' hammering. Then, when all the serious media players ostentatiously withdrew their bids for datacasting spectrum, the same Murdoch newspapers ran alarmist front-page stories claiming that the collapse of the auction would now cause a catastrophic billion-dollar budget black hole. This was the 'wealth and power' side of greatness writ large.

In the end, against the impressive financial achievements of both moguls, we are surely entitled to set the ancient Roman test of *cui bono*: who benefits? The media can only operate on the basis of public trust. In return they have a balancing responsibility to act in the public interest. Can the mighty Packer and Murdoch machines legitimately claim to have served that interest before their own?

It is not as if Australia has had no genuinely 'great' press proprietors on which young Kerry and Rupert might have modelled themselves. For more than a century the Syme and Fairfax families supported their quality newspapers – the Melbourne *Age* and *The Sydney Morning Herald* – with notable courage and a minimum of editorial interference.

During the 1860s, *The Age* led a protracted campaign to break up the vast landholdings of the Victorian squattocracy, then moved on to champion the introduction of free, compulsory and secular education. Those victories set a tradition that still measures the paper's standing by the quality of its journalism rather than the size of its profits.

Four generations later, *The Sydney Morning Herald* was only able to survive the chaos of a disastrously bungled takeover when its staff rebelled against management threats to their professional independence. In a remarkable signal that ethics mattered more to them than the Fairfax share price, the newspaper's own board sided with the editors and journalists and dumped their senior executives.

It would never have happened at News Limited or PBL. ∎

chesty bonds

AKIRA ISOGAWA

I discovered Chesty Bonds for first time in 1986 when I arrived in Australia. It
was at Gowings Centre, on the corner of George and Market Street in Sydney.
This is a uniform construction workers wear, I thought to myself. Though, I later
found out that these are worn by nearly everyone in Australia!

As I have a soft spot for uniforms, I could not resist purchasing one to
wear with my black Yohji Yamamoto trousers. I didn't look quite as tough and
masculine as the construction workers, but I knew they would work well with
my wardrobe. My school friends in Kyoto also started to wear them, as I would
air-post them back home. My friends thought the Chesty Bonds were exciting,
even a touch exotic. I told them they were 'quintessential of Australian style'.
Since then, Chesty Bonds have become one of my favourite gift items.

I could never have imagined back then that I was going to meet up
with the team at Bonds fifteen years later. My collaboration with Bonds started
in October 2001, when I was preparing to show my Spring/Summer 2002
Collection in Paris. I customised the Bonds singlets I used – Chesty and Raglan
– with hand embellishments. When I was fitting the singlets on models before
the show, they all told me how comfortable they felt. I knew this was a good
sign for a commercially successful collection, especially because all the models
were European and a lot of our clients are based in Europe. As suspected, all the
Bonds styles we offered in Paris had an instant positive response.

As for the local market here in Australia, David Jones took an immediate liking to the Bonds range. The Chestys and Raglans were well merchandised amongst my more dressy pieces. This was exciting. But more than this, I found it fascinating to work with a product that provided me with a blank canvas, so-to-speak, where I was able to apply colours and motifs within an 'anything goes' paradigm. This was a liberating experience.

Since that time, Bonds has become an integral part of my Collections. I have printed and embroidered them, applied appliqués and even took to burning the edges of the hemlines to create an 'antique, pre-loved' look.

One of the highlights of my career as an Australian fashion designer was when I met Mr Chesty, Max Whitehead. Max was recruited as the real-life Chesty Bonds model in the 1950s. In 2004 Max was in my show at the Mercedes Australian Fashion Week in the University of Sydney's ethereal MacLaurin Hall. At the time he was 81 years old. For me, it was a heartfelt moment to witness an Australian icon walking down the runway in my show. Max wore a white Chesty Bonds singlet, which had been embroidered with black and white glass beads, displaying the institutional folk hero, 'Mr Chesty'.

By this time I had come to realise that Bonds was in fact adored by people of all ages and different cultural backgrounds, and was an iconic brand that has managed to transcend time. ■

the pub

ROY MASTERS

To misquote William Shakespeare, 'Some pubs are named great, some achieve greatness and some have greatness thrust upon them.' Pubs termed 'great' tend to hug the compass, as in the Great Northern at Byron Bay and the Great Southern in Sydney's Haymarket, a pub I would sneak to for a shower after catching a train down from the bush. You could never call a pub 'Best Western', as in the hotel chain, simply because pubs and hotels are different. Pubs sell beer, while hotels provide beds and meals. Ask a publican for a room upstairs and he'll eye you suspiciously. Ask a hotelier for a beer and he'll lecture you on how mushroom risotto goes better with sav blanc. Pubs are English/Irish and hotels/bars are American.

As Booker Prize-winning author Tom Keneally says, 'Pubs are one of the two founding institutions of the colony, the other one being sodomy.' Today, you can have sex in a pub. The Bulldogs' rugby league forward Sonny Bill Williams achieved congress with a (female) triathlete in the gents' toilet of the Clovelly Hotel in Sydney, and quickly earned the nickname 'Dunny Bill' Williams.

The Clovelly falls into Shakespeare's second category of pubs – it has achieved greatness because it is the de facto headquarters of the National Rugby League. The most important decisions in the code are made at the 'Cloey', as opposed to the official NRL headquarters located at Fox Studios. Leading administrators, coaches, players and journalists gather there to discuss crucial issues, such as the choice of referee for the grand final or the salary cap. Melbourne has its Cloey, although it is spelt Chloey, the name of the nude female whose painting has been hanging in Young and Jackson's pub, opposite Flinders Street Station, since 1909. The iconic Melbourne landmark has also achieved greatness because it is perfectly located as a meeting place. Similarly, the Birdsville Hotel in Australia's outback has achieved greatness.

Shakespeare's third category – the pubs which have had greatness thrust upon them – include the Ettamogah, the cartoon strip which became a pub. Its creator was Ken Maynard, who started drawing the imaginary watering hole in 1959 in the now defunct *Australasian Post* magazine. 'Ettamogah' is allegedly Aboriginal for 'place of good drink', and the comic strip spawned a fair dinkum pub just north of Albury. There are now Ettamogahs west of Sydney, on the Sunshine Coast and east of Perth, making it the most photographed pub in the world.

The best publicans are women. When I grew up on the New South Wales north coast, three ladies – Mrs Ring, Mrs Dickey and Mrs Hole – met midweek for a game of cards and to discuss their mutual problems running pubs. They instinctively understood that a pub is a place where men seek resolution. If you have an unresolved problem with a mate, a pub is the place to settle it, even if required to 'go out the back'. Mrs Ring, who owned the Billinudgel Hotel, a pub where I had my buck's night, lived to 100. Clearly, she knew when to be a diplomat, an autocrat and a doormat. One of Melbourne's best pubs is owned by a 90-year-old woman, Kath Byer. Her Notting Hill establishment services Monash University, and she still sits in a steel cage every morning, counting the previous day's takings. Suzie Carleton ran the Bellevue at Paddington for years, a pub which launched many a book, including those of my mother, Olga Masters, as well as serving as a hub of political activity.

My 50th and 60th birthdays were both held in pubs with John Singleton, the adman turned brewer. Singo threatened to fight the Pommy proprietor at my 50th, held at Phillip's Foot, Australia's first pub, named after Captain Arthur Phillip, Sydney's first governor. Ten years later, Singo had cooled down and we sedately co-celebrated our 60ths at Sydney's Hollywood Hotel, a 1950s style pub chosen to help us recall, rather than recapture, our youth.

You can do almost anything in pubs, including buying an engine block, or an alfoil container of mashed potatoes in order to line your stomach for a heavy day on the syrup, ink, booze, grog or squirt. The one thing you can't do in a pub is fart. Johnny Bruyn once owned one of Armidale's most popular pubs, despite the small size of its public bar. A schoolteacher named Jimmy Stokes, whose vertical hold problems resembled those of the black-and-white TVs of the era, silently broke wind one cold, winter night. Those with an acute sense of smell were first to detect it, sniffing the wind like rabbits, before quickly scooping their change from the counter and bolting for the door. Ex-footballers with broken noses were the last to realise, caught between the desire to finish their schooners and the need to breathe. Bruyn was similarly trapped, knowing his abuse of Stokes would require more intake of oxygen.

The once-great pub no longer exists. ∎

ned kelly

CHESTER PORTER

Ned Kelly was born to an emancipated convict selector in 1885. It was a district of poor Irish selectors, perhaps overly keen on stealing horses and cattle of wealthy squatters, that were subject to severe gaol sentences for their sins. Ned's father and uncle, and many neighbours, were victims of the law. He himself was gaoled twice before the age of 16. The police were hardly friends to this community.

On 15 April 1878, Constable Fitzpatrick, a far from upright policeman who was sacked later in disgrace, returned from a visit to the Kelly home claiming that he had been assaulted by Mrs Kelly and two men and shot in the wrist by Ned. Ned claimed he wasn't even there. His mother and the two men received severe sentences, on very dubious evidence, from Justice Barry. No less than eight policemen, heavily armed but not in uniform, were sent to arrest Ned.

Ned took to the bush in the nearby Wombat Ranges, later to be joined by his brother, Dan, Joe Byrne and Steve Hart. Between them they had one good rifle, held by Ned, and an unreliable gun, which was not used when the police were waylaid at Stringy Bark Creek on 26 October 1878. Ned tried to disarm the police, but they went for their weapons and he killed three of them, Constable Lonigan first, then Sergeant Kennedy and Constable Scanlon last. Constable McIntyre was captured but later escaped. Kelly was outlawed, and the police were entitled to shoot him down without any attempt to arrest him. This had in fact happened, as Ned well knew, to his hero Ben Hall on 6 May 1865.

The local community did not blame Ned and, despite very large reward offers, would not betray him until June 1880, when Joe Byrne's friend, Aaron Sherritt, tried for the reward and was subsequently killed by Joe. Until then the Kelly Gang had been successful bushrangers, carrying out skilful raids on the banks at Euroa on 9 December 1878 and at Jerilderie on 8 February 1879. The large proceeds of these robberies rewarded loyal friends in the community.

By June 1880 they were a weary gang, tired of the constant pursuits and rough living in the bush. They had constructed suits of armour out of ploughshares and, equipped with these, decided to hold Glenrowan Hotel against a large army of police. On 28 June 1880 the police siege resulted in the deaths of every gang member except Ned. He could have escaped but instead, clad in his armour, made a solo attack on the police. Shot in the arms and legs, he was eventually captured. When asked why he did not escape, he replied, 'A man would be a dingo to desert his mates.'

Patched up for his trial, he was refused an adjournment by Justice Barry. His counsel had a late brief and failed to put up any effective defence. Sentenced to death, he told the judge, 'I will see you there.' Visited by his mother, he was told, 'Mind you die like a Kelly, son.'

Right up to until the middle of the twentieth century, in Kelly country Ned was believed to be a victim of injustice. Victorian criminal lawyers, in a mock trial on the evidence some years ago, found him 'not guilty' of the murder charges, on the grounds of self-defence. There was considerable evidence of the police's intention to kill rather than arrest him. Whether that was so or not, Ned Kelly probably did believe that he was going to be shot, with good reason.

Properly represented, he had a good defence – but this evidence was never put to the jury. They were hard days. He was a victim as much as a villain, and his last words reflected resignation to this inescapably cruel reality: 'Such is life.' Ned Kelly was hanged on 11 November 1880. Two days later Justice Barry collapsed. He died on 23 November – 12 days after Ned. To Ned's friends, this karmic event seemed to confirm that Ned did not have a fair trial, as was in fact the case. ■

Australia (in tears)—"MY SONG-BIRD HAS FLOWN AGAIN"

FROM "THE MELBOURNE PUNCH," FEBRUARY 1908

melba

JIM DAVIDSON

Dame Nellie Melba (1861–1931) is probably still unmatched as the most famous Australian of all. Odd, perhaps, that this distinction should go to a singer. But large portions of the world are indifferent to the sports we play, and hence to our celebrated sportspeople. When it comes to Nobel laureates, Patrick White has had less impact abroad than one might expect; our scientists are scarcely household words even at home. In international affairs, Australian politicians cannot be said to have made a sustained contribution – unlike, say, South Africa's Jan Smuts. One day, perhaps, Rupert Murdoch might be considered a contender – but not yet. So Melba it remains.

What then was the nature of this reputation? It was based on a truly phenomenal voice, which moved across three octaves. Melba sang with seeming effortlessness: a rival soprano envied the way her voice rose up from the stage and seemed to hover in the auditorium like a beam of light. A recorded graph of Melba's trill produced over six metres of undulations, between perfectly parallel lines. Moreover, she sought out the famous composers of the day to discuss their music with them, in order to be able to sing it with complete accuracy.

The voice may not have been sufficient in itself. A number of Australian women had gone to Europe and made reputations for themselves; but Melba outshone all the rest of them put together. Apart from hard work and unremitting application, she had an iron will and throughout her life was ruthless with competitors. Melba demanded special treatment at Covent Garden (which she dominated for over thirty years) and, since she delivered the goods, was given her own special dressing room. Even when she was away she kept the key.

Moreover, coached by her Paris teacher Mathilde Marchesi, Melba developed a distinct understanding of the social context in which she was moving. The opera house in the late nineteenth century has been called the cathedral of the bourgeoisie; and Melba comported herself accordingly. Almost effortlessly the Richmond tomboy assumed the grand manner – with just a flicker of defiance. 'There are lots of duchesses,' she told one of them, 'but only one Melba.' Aware of the importance of deportment and good elocution, she never tired of emphasising them to the aspiring young. They would, however, always disappoint. Her particular protégé, Stella Power, was known as the 'Little Melba', then faded away. It was a contradiction in terms.

At the height of her career, in the decades each side of 1900, Melba sang in command performances before Queen Victoria, the German Kaiser, the Austrian Emperor, the Tsar, the President of France, and the King of Sweden. Her one known affair was with the Duke of Orleans, son of the pretender to the French throne. 'Years of almost monotonous brilliance' was how it was summed up in her Covent Garden farewell program.

At the same time, since there was not then the division between popular music and classical that there is now, she was mobbed wherever she went – just like a rock star. Indeed, crowds were unusually familiar with 'the Voice', as Melba sometimes referred to herself, for once won over to sound recording Melba had helped to establish the gramophone. With her instinctive gift for publicity, she insisted on a special label – and a de luxe price.

Not surprisingly for the time, Melba described herself generally as British – never English – sometimes as Australian, and occasionally as Scottish. But at home she was unequivocally regarded as the greatest Australian. To some extent she had put Melbourne on the map, by truncating its name and making it her own (instead of the Nellie Mitchell she was born, or the Mrs Armstrong she was for a time). Her brief return in 1902 was like a royal progress; later in life her series of reluctant farewells, for she was as strong as a horse, went into the language as 'doing a Melba'. Her death in 1931 robbed the country of an icon.

Melba was, beyond the name, a construct. She made a dozen roles her own and, after a few ventures beyond, resolutely stuck to them. Her acting was adequate, rather than inspired. The instrumental purity of the voice was her greatest asset, for at the time such fidelity was particularly admired. Yet the achievement was substantial nonetheless.

Internationally, her name lingers as a symbol of the *belle époque,* and her image still turns up in surprising places – such as on a postage stamp from Nicaragua.

An unintended pathos marked her death. Melba, who had died on the stage many times, now found illusion her undoing. She had had a facelift before leaving England, and while she was in Australia it became septic. In St Vincent's Hospital, Darlinghurst, this monarch of the lyric stage breathed her last. ■

Issued by Authority of THE DEFENCE DEPARTMENT OF THE COMMONWEALTH. —— S.T. LEIGH & Co. Ld LITHOGRAPHIC PRINTERS, SYDNEY.

the expeditionary tradition

RICHARD WHITE

Old soldiers in Australia used to be known – uniquely – as 'returned' men. The term first caught on as Australians came home from the Boer War in 1902. After the Great War of 1914–1918, the war to end all wars, the organisation that came to represent the men who survived would always be known, despite four name changes, as a league of *Returned* Servicemen. The fact that they 'returned' would also define the old soldiers from that still greater war that followed in 1939–1945, and from the Korean War and the Malayan Emergency in the 1950s. It was only with the Vietnam War – and the later involvements in the Gulf, East Timor, Afghanistan and Iraq – that returned men were turned into 'veterans'.

The dominance of the motif of 'return' in Australians' regard for old soldiers says much about Australian understandings of war. War, almost by definition in Australia, is something that happens elsewhere. Australian soldiers traditionally sailed away to fight. Those who survived and returned were regarded as different from the men who had gone away: variously ennobled, traumatised, emboldened, chastened – but always different. It was just as true in the nineteenth century, with those colonial military adventures that Australians joined with such enthusiasm, fighting the Maoris in New Zealand (1860–1869), avenging the death of General Gordon in the Sudan in 1885 and suppressing the Boxer rebellion against foreign control of China.

This 'expeditionary tradition', in which Australians rushed away to fight in other lands, would mark Australia's social and cultural experience of war throughout the twentieth century. There were consistent patterns across all these wars. In no case was Australia directly threatened. Only during World War II, after Japan entered the war in 1941, was there any sense that Australia itself might be a direct target. But in 1939, when committing to the war, Australia was at war by proxy: as Menzies put it, Britain had declared war on Germany and as a consequence Australia was also at war.

That's not to say, necessarily, that Australia was simply fighting other people's wars. It reflected rather Australians' particular outlook on the rest of the world. Isolated in what they regarded as a generally hostile world, far from those nations they most identified with, Australians readily looked to 'great and powerful friends' – Britain first and then the United States. Other voices argued for more nuanced, multilateral approaches, but using Australian troops to bolster a patron's role in world affairs was a logical if somewhat cynical approach to geopolitics. Australians could congratulate themselves that they had always found themselves on the side – if not of right – always of might and of white, from the Darwinian superiority of white civilisation fighting Maoris to the 'shock and awe' that the world's greatest military power could mobilise in Iraq.

The expeditionary tradition had a number of consequences. First, it gave Australians an unrealistic understanding of war. War has always been a distant affair, leaving few scars on the Australian landscape. There has been no instance of a standing army firing on civilians, no experience of civil war, no invading armies raping or pillaging, no cities destroyed: only Indigenous Australians have fought a land war against invaders. The focus on war as necessarily distant helped non-Aboriginal Australians forget the long tragedy of disease, murder, disintegration and open warfare by which Aboriginal people were dispossessed.

The distancing unreality of the expeditionary tradition also meant war could be associated not with carnage but with adventure and seeing the world.

The rush to enlist in 1914 was stimulated not just by the sense of imperial duty instilled in school children but a sense of adventure for 'six-bob-a-day tourists'. It was, as one recruitment leaflet put it, a 'free trip to Europe' for men who, though brought up to regard Europe as the cultural centre of their world, would otherwise have had no chance of travelling outside Australia.

The prospect of adventure meant recruitment could be voluntary long after other armies filled their ranks with conscripts, and the fundamentally voluntary nature of these expeditions gave them particular esteem. Only in less attractive Asian theatres, at the end of World War II and in Vietnam, did governments need to resort to conscription. In any case, from Korea on, the professional regular army – which had been so scorned by the volunteer troops of the two world wars – was given the responsibility for fighting Australia's wars. Only after vigorous public relations efforts in the late twentieth century could the regular army lay claim to what had always been a vehemently civilian-based Anzac tradition.

And above all the expeditionary tradition created a mythology around Anzac, which drew much from the fact that the dead were buried so far from home. War memorials in Australia took on the emotional role of substitute graves, around which developed an elaborate civil religion depicting the dead as heroes and women – mothers, sisters, wives – as mourners. As a national myth it excluded many: those that resisted the 'call of stoush', the generations that inconveniently came of age between major wars, migrants arriving after the fighting. Perhaps that was its role. Even those who fought and returned could be ambivalent about the myth-making: some thrived on their annual elevation to hero status, others found the posturing of politicians on Anzac Day hollow. The gap between those who had seen war and a society so distant from it was always difficult to bridge, though many slipped easily into pre-war lives. Others, generation after generation of those who went away to fight, would always feel that the society they returned to failed them. ∎

water dreaming

HETTI PERKINS

The remote outback community of Walungurru (Kintore) lies 530 kilometres to the west of Mparntwe (Alice Springs). This desert outpost in the Pintupi heartlands is a seven-hour four-wheel drive trip when the dirt track is dry and a seemingly interminable, treacherous one when the rains turn the corrugations and dust bowl verges into a slippery quagmire. Still, it's one of the most amazing expeditions on offer – with land council permission – for both its historical interest and wonderful vistas.

About a third of the way down the track, after leaving the bitumen route to Yuendumu, the road enters Papunya. This community, named for the honey ant ancestors that entered the earth at this site, also lent its name to the internationally renowned Aboriginal artists' company established in 1971. Today, there is no civic recognition of the remarkable genesis of Papunya Tula Artists, and most of the company stakeholders and artist members have returned home, westwards to outstations and communities like Walungurru, founded in the post-Land Rights Act era of the late 1970s and early 80s. Yet, a walk around the back of the community store brings into view two unassuming derelict hangars. Adjoined to one is the old bakery oven, suggesting that this was once the 'painting shed' where the artists and avid supporter Geoffrey Bardon congregated to create art from the detritus of the white community, a product of their cultural heritage and their inheritance as the fringe-dwellers of the government's assimilation project.

One of the surviving founders of Papunya Tula Artists, the dearly loved Long Jack Phillipus Tjakamarra, still lives in Papunya and only intermittently paints. While the company field officers these days rarely pause on their way west, a fledgling arts collective, Papunya Tjupi, has emerged at Papunya, bringing a renewed vigour to the community. Upon leaving Papunya, the heavens open up, mirroring the immensity of the continent along whose horizon weather changes can be monitored over hundreds of kilometres. Gradually Yunytju, the dramatic range that marks the approach of Walungurru, appears, drawing to its peak the rains that give the community its unique ecology and comparatively reliable water table.

The story of the desert people is one marked by resilience and initiative; seen in the exploitation of government or mission resources in times of drought or massacre, the return to their homelands, the establishment of arts enterprises and health services, and most recently the fundraising effort to build a swimming pool in Walungurru.

Flying to Walungurru for the pool opening on 1 February 2008 by charter plane was a two-hour trip gliding over some of the most dramatic landscape on the continent. After the Western MacDonnell Ranges, the flight path took us past vast salt lakes and myriad landforms that mark the presence of ancestors in this sentient country. Punctuated at its beginning and end by the turbulence generated by abruptly rising landforms out of the desert plain, an almost opaque haze veils our destination, causing some anxiety to the pilot – and passengers – as landings here are by sight. We successfully negotiated Yunytju and headed to the newly erected art centre complex with the Papunya Tula staff. From the shade of the studio veranda, the new pool could be seen in the township centre, flanked by the school, clinic, store and council offices.

On this suitably blisteringly hot day in one of the most arid places on earth, a troupe of benefactors, government bureaucrats and media joined the community and legions of barely restrained children to open the newly constructed Yunytju Pulikutjarra Pool. Funded by an art auction featuring specially commissioned paintings by five senior Papunya Tula artists, the opening formalities were concluded by one of them, Ronnie Tjampitjinpa, who cut the ribbon across its entry. Swarms of excited children immediately overran guests and locals as they poured into the change rooms and out to the pool. Attendants vainly attempted to enforce the shower rules, dropping dobs of shampoo on each little head as the tidal wave of children surged through the building.

The wish to have a swimming pool in Walungurru was probably as old as the community itself; however for me it began during a conversation with Daphne Williams, long-term manager of Papunya Tula Artists. About ten years ago we were sitting in the old gallery premises in Mparntwe talking about the major exhibition planned for the Art Gallery of New South Wales in 2000: *Papunya Tula: Genesis and Genius*. I clearly remember Daphne sharing with me her dream of a swimming pool for all the children in the community she had faithfully served, traversing thousands of kilometres in an old ute for over a decade. As she couldn't attend the opening, I could only imagine how she would have felt watching the pool rapidly fill to standing room only and her successor, Paul Sweeney, proudly proclaim himself as the 'first whitefella in' – a fitting tribute to a person who also played an instrumental role in the fundraising effort.

After retreating to the calm of the temporarily abandoned art centre, I reflected that, like the paintings of the artists, this pool represents so much more than its face value. The paintings are not just things of beauty, wonderful designs that dazzle us with their artistic brilliance. They are title deeds to country; they are histories of countless generations of people, of ancestors who created and named this country. This wonderful new swimming pool is more than a place to have fun. It is also about family and country. It is clinically proven what a critical difference swimming pools make to the physical and mental health of all people of all ages in remote communities. Like the Western Desert Dialysis organisation, this swimming pool is another example of Aboriginal resourcefulness to make remote area community life sustainable and to support our people to live in 21st-century Australia in a culturally appropriate way.

At the closure of a historic day, I was told at the art centre that the haze earlier in the day had been caused by the Kungka Kutjarra, the two ancestral women of the Tjukurrpa who had followed the old man Yunytju, and passed through the Walungurru ranges known as Pulikutjarra. The pounding of their digging sticks into the earth to express their endorsement of the new water source at Walungurru had created the swirling dust clouds, eventually subsiding with due ceremony to unveil a contemporary landmark in Pintupi country. ■

(The author would like to thank Murphy Roberts Tjupurrula. The Pool Party fundraiser was held at the Art Gallery of New South Wales on 3 November 2005 and supported by the Charlie Perkins Children's Trust.)

list of contributors

ROBYN ARCHER is a singer, writer and artistic director, formerly of the major festivals in Adelaide, Melbourne, Canberra, Tasmania and currently of The Light in Winter (Melbourne) and adviser to Luminato (Toronto). Her new play, *Architektin*, will premiere in 2008.

MAGGIE BEER is a South Australian cook, food author, restaurateur, food manufacturer and television host. She currently operates a business in the Barossa that produces a range of specialty gourmet foods, including Pheasant Farm Pate, quince paste, verjuice and ice creams.

TIM BOWDEN is a broadcaster, radio and television documentary maker, oral historian and author. He worked as a foreign correspondent in Asia and North America in the 1960s, founded the ABC's Social History Unit in 1985 and presently enjoys an active retirement writing travel books.

VERONICA BRADY is an honorary Senior Research Fellow in the Department of English and Cultural Studies at the University of Western Australia. She is also a Roman Catholic nun, a member of the Loreto Order.

JUDITH BRETT teaches politics at La Trobe University and has written extensively on the Australian Liberal Party, including her prize-winning book *Robert Menzies' Forgotten People*. First published in 1992, a second edition was published by Melbourne University Press in 2007.

CARLOTTA is an icon of Australian cabaret, celebrating forty years in the business. She began her career in the 1960s as one of the original members of the internationally renowned Les Girls in Sydney's King Cross.

PETER COCHRANE is a freelance writer based in Sydney. His last book, *Colonial Ambition: Foundations of Australian Democracy* was the 2007 *Age* Book of the Year and co-winner of the Inaugural Prime Minister's Prize for Australian History.

ANN CURTHOYS is Manning Clark Professor of History at the Australian National University. She has written many articles and books about history, especially Australian history, including *Freedom Ride: A Freedom Rider Remembers*.

JIM DAVIDSON is an honorary fellow of the School of Historical Studies, University of Melbourne. He is the author of the prize-winning biography *Lyrebird Rising: Louise Hanson-Dyer of Oiseau-Lyre*.

TONY DAVIS is the author of the eccentric literary memoir *F. Scott, Ernest and Me*, the bestselling *Lemon! Sixty Heroic Failures of Motoring*, and books for children including the Roland Wright, Future Knight series. He has written extensively about popular culture, travel, history, music and motoring for local and international newspapers and magazines.

ROLF de HEER is an Adelaide-based film director, writer and producer. His 1996 film *Ten Canoes* won numerous awards, including the Australian Film Institute's Best Film, Best Direction and Best Original Screenplay.

JOHN EDWARDS has been Chief Economist at HSBC in Australia since early 1997. He holds a PhD in Economics from George Washington University and is the author of three books, including *Keating* – a bestselling biography of the former Prime Minister.

MIRIAM ESTENSEN is the author of several books and articles on Australian maritime history, including *The Life of Matthew Flinders* and most recently *Terra Australis Incognita: The Spanish Quest for the Mysterious Great South Land*. Widely travelled, she now lives on Australia's Gold Coast.

MATTHEW EVANS is a former chef by trade who turned food writer by desire. Once a food critic in our largest city, the author of several books on food now lives the real life in Tasmania, dividing his time between foraging for food in both shops and the bush and trying to work a wood-fired stove.

ELIZABETH FARRELLY is a multi-award-winning Sydney writer, columnist for *The Sydney Morning Herald* and Adjunct Associate Professor of Architecture at the University of Sydney. Her books include *Three Houses: Glenn Murcutt* and *Blubberland: The Dangers of Happiness*.

MARTIN FLANAGAN is an author and journalist. He has written twelve books, including *The Call*, an imaginary reconstruction of the life of Tom Wills, a founder of Australian football.

ANGELA GOODE is well-known for the bestselling *Great Working Dog Stories* books. She has been a columnist since 1981 for *The Advertiser* and broadcasts for ABC radio on rural life and issues. She lives on a beef-cattle farm near Naracoorte in South Australia.

LINCOLN HALL is Australia's most accomplished mountaineering writer, whose high-altitude climbing career culminated in his key role in the first Australian ascent of Mt Everest in 1984. His eighth book, *Dead Lucky*, tells of his harrowing near-death experience on Everest in 2006.

ASHLEY HAY has written four books of narrative non-fiction – *The Secret* and *Gum*, and *Herbarium* and *Museum* (both with photographer Robyn Stacey) – as well as essays, short stories and journalism.

JOHN HIRST is a historian attached to La Trobe University in Melbourne and the University of Sydney. He is the author of *The Sentimental Nation: The Making of the Australian Commonwealth*.

ROBYN HOLMES is Curator of Music at the National Library of Australia. She has researched and published extensively on Australian musical culture and pioneered national collaborative projects, including the online Music Australia service.

AKIRA ISOGAWA is one of Australia's most prominent contemporary fashion designers. Born in Japan and immigrating to Australia in 1986, Akira's collections are sold around the world.

BARRY JONES, who knew Mac Burnet, is a politician, writer and broadcaster, who was Minister for Science (1983–1990) and represented Australia at UNESCO (1991–1995). He is a fellow of all four Australian learned academies.

TOM KENEALLY is the multi-award-winning author of twenty-six works of fiction, most notably the Booker Prize-winning *Schindler's Ark*, and nine works of non-fiction. He is married with two daughters and three grandchildren.

DR MOHAMED KHADRA is a former professor of surgery who is now president and co-founder of the Institute of Technology Australia. He is the author of *Making the Cut*, an account of his life as a surgeon, and has a book about the ordeal of illness called *The Patient* due for publication in March 2009.

PETER KIRKPATRICK writes poetry and cultural history, and teaches Australian Literature in the School of Letters, Art & Media at the University of Sydney. He is the author of *The Sea Coast of Bohemia: Literary Life in Sydney's Roaring Twenties*.

MARCIA LANGTON was appointed Foundation Professor of Australian Indigenous Studies at the University of Melbourne in early 2000. She has many years' experience working as an anthropologist in indigenous affairs with governments and universities. She is currently Chair of the Cape York Institute for Policy and Leadership.

SYLVIA LAWSON writes essays, history and fiction. Her work includes *The Archibald Paradox*, on the early Sydney *Bulletin* and its first editor, and T*he Outside Story*, a novel centred on the early history of the Sydney Opera House.

KATHY LETTE first achieved *succès de scandale* as a teenager with the novel *Puberty Blues*. She has written ten bestselling books and is now published in seventeen languages in over 100 countries. Her latest novel is *To Love, Honour and Betray – Till Divorce Us Do Part.*

SARAH MACDONALD is a writer, journalist and radio broadcaster based in Sydney. Her bestselling book *Holy Cow! An Indian Adventure* has sold in the UK and US and been translated into Dutch and German, and she edited the travel collections *Come Away With Me* and *Take Me With You.*

ROSS McMULLIN is a historian whose books include the award-winning biography *Pompey Elliott* (republished by Scribe with a foreword by Les Carlyon) and *Will Dyson: Australia's Radical Genius.*

HUMPHREY McQUEEN is a Canberra aged pensioner who swims, sees a lot of movies, researches builders' labourers and subverts the rule of capital.

STEPHEN MARTIN is an Antarctic historian and tour guide with extensive research experience in the Antarctic collections of the State Library of NSW.

ROY MASTERS is a former rugby league coach with Western Suburbs and St George and writes for *The Sydney Morning Herald*. He also appears on Channel Two's *Offsiders* program.

TIM MURRAY is Professor of Archaeology and Head of the School of Historical and European Studies at La Trobe University. His research focuses on historical archaeology and theoretical issues, but his most recent book is a single-volume history of archaeology, *Milestones in Archaeology.*

HETTI PERKINS is a member of the Eastern Arrernte and Kalkadoon Aboriginal communities. Currently the Senior Curator of Aboriginal and Torres Strait Islander Art at the Art Gallery of NSW in Sydney, she has worked with indigenous visual art for over twenty years.

CHESTER PORTER QC was a barrister for 52 years, appearing in many famous criminal cases. Retiring from the Bar on 30 June 2000, the Bar Council of NSW made him an Honorary Life Member in August 2000 for his exceptional service to the Bar and the profession of law.

JULIE RIGG is a writer, broadcaster and ABC Radio National's specialist film critic. In 2003 she was awarded the Pascall Prize for critical writing.

MARGOT RILEY is a cultural historian with special interest in textiles and dress. Her professional experience includes curatorial positions with the Powerhouse Museum and the Historic Houses Trust of NSW, and she is currently based at the State Library of NSW.

GEOFFREY ROBERTSON QC, a graduate of Sydney University and a Rhodes Scholar, has appeared in many landmark human rights cases in courts around the world. He was the first President of the United Nations War Crimes Court in Sierra Leone and is now a member of the United Nations International Justice Council. His most recent book is *The Tyrannicide Brief.*

HAZEL ROWLEY is the author of *Christina Stead: A Biography* (1994 Australian National Book Council Award), *Richard Wright: The Life and Times* (*Washington Post* Best Book) and *Tête à Tête: Simone de Beauvoir and Jean-Paul Sartre* (translated into fourteen languages). She resides in New York City.

TIM ROWSE, an academic social scientist and historian with a particular interest in indigenous affairs, will join the Whitlam Centre for Citizenship and Public Policy, University of Western Sydney, in January 2009. He has written two books about Nugget Coombs: *Obliged to Be Difficult* and *Nugget: A Reforming Life.*

DAVID SALTER is a veteran independent journalist and television producer. He was Executive Producer of ABC-TV's *Media Watch* for five years and writes regularly on media issues for *The Australian.*

PETER SPEARRITT first walked over the main arch of the Bridge in 1981, seventeen years before BridgeClimb started charging people for the same thrill. His biography *The Sydney Harbour Bridge: A Life*, published for the bridge's 50th anniversary in 1982, was revised for the 75th anniversary in 2007.

PETER STANLEY is Director of the Centre for Historical Research at the National Museum of Australia. He has just published *Invading Australia: Japan and the Battle for Australia 1942,* and is finishing a book on the lives of members of an Australian platoon that fought at Mont St Quentin.

DAVID STRATTON is a former director of the Sydney Film Festival, former film critic for the international film industry magazine *Variety* and is currently film critic for *The Australian*. A recipient of the Australian Film Institute's Raymond Longford Award, David is the co-host of *At the Movies* on ABC.

HUGH STRETTON, brought up in the seaside suburb of Beaumaris, Victoria, learned and taught history, political science and economics in the UK, the US and for most of his working life in Adelaide. His latest books are *Economics: A New Introduction* and *Australia Fair*.

RACHAEL TREASURE lives on a sheep and cattle farm in Tasmania with her husband, John, and two children. She is the author of the novels *Jillaroo, The Stockmen* and *The Rouseabout*, the SBSi screenplay *Albert's Chook Tractor* and two ebooks.

RUTH WAJNRYB is an applied linguist, researcher and writer, with a weekly column ('Words') in the weekend *Sydney Morning Herald*. Her most recent book is *Cheerio Tom, Dick and Harry: Despatches from the Hostel of Fading Words*.

ELIZABETH WEBBY is Emeritus Professor of Australian Literature at the University of Sydney. Her publications include *The Cambridge Companion to Australian Literature*.

RICHARD WHITE teaches in the Department of History, University of Sydney, and has written on the relationship between war and tourism. His books include *Inventing Australia, The Oxford Book of Australian Travel Writing* (co-editor) and *On Holidays: A History of Getting Away in Australia*.

A William Heinemann book
Published by Random House Australia Pty Ltd
Level 3, 100 Pacific Highway, North Sydney NSW 2060
www.randomhouse.com.au

First published by William Heinemann in 2008

Addresses for companies within the Random House Group can be found at www.randomhouse.com.au/offices.
Australian greats/editor: Peter Cochrane.

ISBN 978 1 74166 592 5 (hbk.)

National characteristics, Australian.
Nationalism – Australia.
Collective memory – Australia.
Australia – Social life and customs.
Cochrane, Peter, 1950–.

305.800994

Cover and internal design by i2i Design Pty Ltd
Typeset by i2i Design Pty Ltd
Printed and bound by i Book Printing Ltd, China

S McMULLIN TIM MURRAY JULIE RIGG LINCOLN HALL **MARGOT RILEY** ELIZABETH WEBBY JOHN HIRST JOHN E
CURTHOYS **HAZEL ROWLEY** KATHY LETTE MOHAMED KHADRA DAVID STRATTON HUMPHREY McQUEEN TIM BO
RY JONES DAVID SALTER AKIRA ISOGAWA ROY MASTERS CHESTER PORTER JIM DAVIDSON RICHARD WHITE HE
GTON TONY DAVIS ASHLEY HAY TOM KENEALLY PETER KIRKPATRICK MATTHEW EVANS ROBYN ARCHER PETER
ARDS HUGH STRETTON ROBYN HOLMES ROLF de HEER JUDITH BRETT PETER SPEARRITT MARTIN FLANAGAN
DEN TIM ROWSE VERONICA BRADY SARAH MACDONALD RACHAEL TREASURE GEOFFREY ROBERTSON MAGGIE
TI PERKINS ANGELA GOODE **ELIZABETH FARRELLY** MIRIAM ESTENSEN PETER STANLEY SYLVIA LAWSON RUTH
HRANE ROSS McMULLIN TIM MURRAY JULIE RIGG LINCOLN HALL MARGOT RILEY ELIZABETH WEBBY JOHN HI
TIN ANN CURTHOYS HAZEL ROWLEY KATHY LETTE MOHAMED KHADRA **DAVID STRATTON** HUMPHREY McQUEE
LOTTA BARRY JONES DAVID SALTER AKIRA ISOGAWA ROY MASTERS CHESTER PORTER JIM DAVIDSON RICHARD
CIA LANGTON TONY DAVIS ASHLEY HAY **TOM KENEALLY** PETER KIRKPATRICK MATTHEW EVANS **ROBYN ARCHE**
ARDS HUGH STRETTON ROBYN HOLMES ROLF de HEER JUDITH BRETT PETER SPEARRITT MARTIN FLANAGAN
DEN TIM ROWSE VERONICA BRADY SARAH MACDONALD RACHAEL TREASURE GEOFFREY ROBERTSON MAGGIE
KINS ANGELA GOODE ELIZABETH FARRELLY MIRIAM ESTENSEN PETER STANLEY SYLVIA LAWSON RUTH WAJNF
HRANE ROSS McMULLIN TIM MURRAY JULIE RIGG **LINCOLN HALL** MARGOT RILEY ELIZABETH WEBBY JOHN HI
TIN ANN CURTHOYS HAZEL ROWLEY KATHY LETTE MOHAMED KHADRA DAVID STRATTON **HUMPHREY McQUEE**
LOTTA BARRY JONES DAVID SALTER AKIRA ISOGAWA ROY MASTERS CHESTER PORTER JIM DAVIDSON RICHARD
CIA LANGTON TONY DAVIS ASHLEY HAY TOM KENEALLY PETER KIRKPATRICK MATTHEW EVANS ROBYN ARCHER
ARDS HUGH STRETTON **ROBYN HOLMES** ROLF de HEER JUDITH BRETT PETER SPEARRITT MARTIN FLANAGAN
DEN TIM ROWSE VERONICA BRADY SARAH MACDONALD RACHAEL TREASURE GEOFFREY ROBERTSON MAGGIE
KINS ANGELA GOODE ELIZABETH FARRELLY MIRIAM ESTENSEN PETER STANLEY **SYLVIA LAWSON** RUTH WAJN
HRANE ROSS McMULLIN TIM MURRAY JULIE RIGG LINCOLN HALL MARGOT RILEY ELIZABETH WEBBY JOHN HI
TIN ANN CURTHOYS HAZEL ROWLEY KATHY LETTE MOHAMED KHADRA DAVID STRATTON HUMPHREY McQUEE
LOTTA BARRY JONES **DAVID SALTER** AKIRA ISOGAWA ROY MASTERS CHESTER PORTER JIM DAVIDSON RICHARD
CIA LANGTON TONY DAVIS ASHLEY HAY TOM KENEALLY **PETER KIRKPATRICK** MATTHEW EVANS ROBYN ARCHE
ARDS HUGH STRETTON ROBYN HOLMES ROLF de HEER JUDITH BRETT PETER SPEARRITT MARTIN FLANAGAN
DEN TIM ROWSE VERONICA BRADY SARAH MACDONALD RACHAEL TREASURE GEOFFREY ROBERTSON **MAGGIE**
TI PERKINS ANGELA GOODE ELIZABETH FARRELLY MIRIAM ESTENSEN PETER STANLEY SYLVIA LAWSON RUTH
HRANE **ROSS McMULLIN** TIM MURRAY JULIE RIGG LINCOLN HALL MARGOT RILEY ELIZABETH WEBBY JOHN H
TIN ANN CURTHOYS HAZEL ROWLEY KATHY LETTE **MOHAMED KHADRA** DAVID STRATTON HUMPHREY McQUEE
LOTTA BARRY JONES DAVID SALTER AKIRA ISOGAWA ROY MASTERS CHESTER PORTER JIM DAVIDSON RICHARD
CIA LANGTON TONY DAVIS ASHLEY HAY TOM KENEALLY PETER KIRKPATRICK MATTHEW EVANS ROBYN ARCHE
ARDS HUGH STRETTON ROBYN HOLMES ROLF de HEER **JUDITH BRETT** PETER SPEARRITT **MARTIN FLANAGAN**
DEN **TIM ROWSE** VERONICA BRADY SARAH MACDONALD RACHAEL TREASURE GEOFFREY ROBERTSON MAGGIE
TI PERKINS ANGELA GOODE ELIZABETH FARRELLY MIRIAM ESTENSEN PETER STANLEY SYLVIA LAWSON RUTH
HRANE ROSS McMULLIN TIM MURRAY JULIE RIGG LINCOLN HALL MARGOT RILEY **ELIZABETH WEBBY** JOHN H
TIN ANN CURTHOYS HAZEL ROWLEY KATHY LETTE MOHAMED KHADRA DAVID STRATTON HUMPHREY McQUEE
LOTTA BARRY JONES DAVID SALTER **AKIRA ISOGAWA** ROY MASTERS CHESTER PORTER JIM DAVIDSON **RICHAR**
CIA LANGTON TONY DAVIS ASHLEY HAY TOM KENEALLY PETER KIRKPATRICK MATTHEW EVANS ROBYN ARCHE
ARDS **HUGH STRETTON** ROBYN HOLMES ROLF de HEER JUDITH BRETT PETER SPEARRITT MARTIN FLANAGAN
DEN TIM ROWSE VERONICA BRADY SARAH MACDONALD RACHAEL TREASURE GEOFFREY ROBERTSON MAGGIE
KINS ANGELA GOODE ELIZABETH FARRELLY MIRIAM ESTENSEN PETER STANLEY SYLVIA LAWSON RUTH WAJN
HRANE ROSS McMULLIN TIM MURRAY JULIE RIGG LINCOLN HALL MARGOT RILEY ELIZABETH WEBBY JOHN H
TIN ANN CURTHOYS HAZEL ROWLEY KATHY LETTE MOHAMED KHADRA DAVID STRATTON HUMPHREY McQUEE
LOTTA BARRY JONES DAVID SALTER AKIRA ISOGAWA ROY MASTERS CHESTER PORTER JIM DAVIDSON RICHARD
CIA LANGTON TONY DAVIS **ASHLEY HAY** TOM KENEALLY PETER KIRKPATRICK MATTHEW EVANS ROBYN ARCHE
ARDS HUGH STRETTON ROBYN HOLMES **ROLF de HEER** JUDITH BRETT PETER SPEARRITT MARTIN FLANAGAN
DEN TIM ROWSE VERONICA BRADY SARAH MACDONALD RACHAEL TREASURE GEOFFREY ROBERTSON MAGGIE